# Plant my feet on
# HIGHER GROUND

Victor M. Matthews

**Original text material by Victor M. Matthews
Developed by Emmaus Correspondence School
which is an extension ministry of
Emmaus Bible College
founded in 1941**

56789/5432109876

Printed in United States of America

# Instructions to Students

PERSONAL SUCCESS—That's the promise of God! "And ye shall know the truth, and the truth shall make you free" (John 8:32).

This *Freedom* is simply personal success for the Christian. It is the liberty, the ability, the right to become the kind of person that God had in mind when He created you. Instead of being enslaved by our sin, crippled by our ignorance, and bound by our tensions—God has promised *Freedom*.

The *Truth* shall make you *Free!* God has revealed the *Truth* to us through the Person of His Son Jesus Christ and it's recorded in the Bible. There is no need to stumble, grope, and guess about the *Truth*.

To *Know* the *Truth* will make us *Free*. Knowledge—Truth—Freedom—these head the list of any system of values. And that's the reason for this course. You can *Know* the *Truth* and you can have the *Freedom* of the personal success. If you will honestly study the Bible and consistently apply it to your daily life—God will transform you as a person. The material you hold in your hand has been carefully prepared to lead you step by step into the *Knowledge* of the *Truth* which will make you *Free!*

## HOW THIS COURSE IS ORGANIZED

1. The Nature of Biblical Christianity
2. The Nature of Biblical Christianity (Cont.)
3. The Characteristics of Biblical Christianity
4. The Application of Biblical Christianity
5. The Biblical Provision for Sanctification
6. The Crucifixion in the Believer's Daily Life
7. The Resurrection in the Believer's Daily Life
8. The Ascension in the Believer's Daily Life

9.  Pentecost in the Believer's Daily Life
10.  "And Now Faith Is . . . "
11.  "And Now Faith Demands . . . "

## HOW TO STUDY

Begin by asking God to open your heart to receive the truths He would teach you from His Word. Read the lesson through at least twice, once to get the general drift of its contents and then again, slowly, looking up all Scripture references and examining all footnotes.

## EXAMS

There is an exam after lesson 1. Thereafter there is an exam after every second lesson—after lessons 3, 5, 7, 9 and 11. Each exam is clearly marked to show you which questions deal with which lesson. You may take the exam in two stages. When you have completed a lesson, you may take the part of the exam dealing with that lesson. Do not mail the exam to the School, however, until you have completed the next lesson and taken the second part of the exam. *NEVER SEND IN AN EXAM FOR CORRECTION UNTIL BOTH PARTS ARE COMPLETED.* Send in an exam for correction as soon as you have completed all of it.

You may use any version of the Bible for general study. When answering exam questions, however, restrict yourself to either the *Authorized (King James) Version (1611),* or the *New American Standard Bible (NASB).* These are two widely used versions. There are so many versions today that your instructor cannot possibly check them all in evaluating your work.

### 1.  Thought and Research Questions

Some exams contain questions designed to make you do original Bible study. You may use your Bible to answer these questions. They are clearly marked.

## 2. What Do You Say? Questions

Questions headed in this way are optional and no point value is assigned to them. You may freely state your own opinions in answer to such questions. Your candid answers will help your instructor get to know you better as an individual. They will also help us evaluate the general effectiveness of this course.

## 3. How Your Papers Are Graded

Any incorrectly answered questions will be marked by your instructor. You will be referred back to the place in the Bible or the textbook where the correct answer is to be found.

## RECORD YOUR GRADES

When you send in your first exam a Grade Record Card will be returned to you showing your grade for the lesson(s) just corrected. You must return this card to the School each time you send in further exams.

## GROUP ENROLLMENTS

If you are enrolled in a class, submit your exam papers to the leader or secretary of the class who will send them for the entire group to the Correspondence School.

## GENERAL INSTRUCTIONS

Begin studying immediately, or, if you are in a group, as soon as the group begins. Try to keep a regular study schedule. Endeavor to complete one lesson every two weeks. This will enable you to complete the course in three months. You may, however, prefer to complete an exam each week and the course in six weeks! Arrange a study schedule that is best suited to you. You will be allowed a maximum of one year to complete this course from the time of enrollment.

# The Nature of Biblical Christianity

## A DISTURBING QUESTION:
### "Do I know what Biblical Christianity is?"

It is very possible for an earnest Christian to be so poorly taught and to so misunderstand the truths of Christianity that he is unable to adequately practice the Christian life.

One of the major sources of weakness, disappointment, and frustration in the life of the Christian stems from failure to understand the nature of Biblical Christianity. What we do not know we cannot practice or enjoy. True worship is governed by truth and the truth must be learned.

Those who work with the laws of physics must know their field. They must learn the nature and characteristics of the laws which pertain to their area of specialization. It is not sufficient to guess. There is no substitute for knowledge in the life of the engineer, the physicist, the mathematician, or the physician. Nor is it enough for the young man to have a desire to build a bridge. He must learn the laws which govern bridge-building and how to put these laws into practice.

The Christian, likewise, must have more than a desire to live successfully. The desire, no matter how great, is not enough. As the engineer, he must learn the truths of Christianity and how to put them into practice. Only then will he have the conditions which will enable him to live successfully.

One important factor which has led to a misunderstanding of Christianity is the failure to distinguish between Biblical principle and "Christian" practice. What Christians and churches practice is not necessarily the truth. One must learn to evaluate even the proclamation of Christians and churches by the principles and truths of the Bible. Many Christians and non-Christians have been confused by poor teaching and poor practice.

It is well to ask the question, "Do I know what Biblical Christianity is?" There are many who are not willing to ask such a question and there are many more who cannot give an adequate answer.

Any hesitancy in this area can only lead to failure.

## A BASIC ASSUMPTION:
### Christianity is Based on Divine Revelation.

Christianity has not been given to us as a lump of clay which may be molded into innumerable shapes. God has revealed Himself to us in and through Jesus Christ. This revelation forms the foundation, the structure, and the content of genuine Christianity. It comes to us as final authority.

Since genuine Christianity is the result of an authoritative revelation, it is evident that any tampering with, or any faulty interpretation of, its basic message can only result in the production of a false Christianity. It is obvious, as one looks about the religious world today, that this is exactly what has happened.

The importance of this assumption can hardly be over-emphasized. The authority for belief and practice is divine revelation. This authority, therefore, does not reside in the church, nor in the leaders of the church, nor in religious experience, whether it be personal or corporate. God is Truth and He has made Himself and His will known. This revelation has been authoritatively recorded in the Scriptures.

To be a genuine Christian and to live a successful Christian life, we must begin, as an engineer, with the acceptance of a final authority. We must bow in complete submission before God and His revelation. No engineer may select the laws which meet his approval and reject the rest. To be successful he must accept all the laws and their authoritative demands. And so it is with the Christian.

Untold damage has resulted due to the negligence of engineers, physicians, and men in similar professions. Far greater damage is to be found in the spiritual realm. Men and women have based their lives and destinies on false interpretations of the Bible. Life, talent, time and money have been wasted. Freedom, power and progress follow the knowledge and practice of the truth. When truth is not known and ignorance is practiced, only harm can follow.

God has made Himself known to us in Jesus Christ, through history, as recorded in the Scripture. This is where we must start. We must be willing to go to this final authority and to test our belief and practice.

God has revealed Himself in two ways—by means of general revelation and by means of special revelation. By *general* revelation we mean those evidences within the creation such as design, stability of law, human values, and conscience which point to the Creator (Psalm 19:1; Romans 1:20; 2:14, 15). God has revealed Himself in His work.

By *special* revelation we refer to the many communications of divine truths whereby God has revealed Himself as the Redeemer of His people. This process of special revelation culminated in the incarnation of Jesus Christ as the living Word, and the completion of the written Word, the Bible (Hebrews 1:1-3; 1 Corinthians 15:1-4). Unless otherwise stated, the term *revelation* is used in these lessons to indicate spiritual revelation.

*The key to success:* accept and obey the revelation of God as final authority.

## AN IMPORTANT PERSPECTIVE:
### Christianity Revolves Around a Person, Jesus Christ.

In the Old Testament days it was the pre-incarnate Christ who said to Abraham, " . . . *I* am thy shield, and thy exceeding great reward" (Genesis 15:1). He said to Moses, " . . . certainly *I* will be with

3

thee . . ." (Exodus 3:12). He spoke to Israel by Hosea and said, " . . . in *Me* is thine help" (Hosea 13:9). Through Jeremiah He spoke to Judah and said, " . . . they have forsaken *Me* the fountain of living waters . . ." (Jeremiah 2:13).

The message of the New Testament is the same. The Lord Jesus Christ said to Peter and Andrew, " . . . Follow *Me* . . ." (Matthew 4:19). He said, "Come unto *Me* . . . and *I* will give you rest" (Matthew 11:28). He also said, " . . . *I* am the light of the world . . ." (John 8:12); " . . . *I* am the resurrection, and the life . . ." (John 11:25); " . . . *I* am the way, the truth, and the life . . ." (John 14:6); " . . . without *Me* ye can do nothing" (John 15:5).

The same emphasis is found in the apostolic interpretation of Christianity. John said, "But as many as received *Him*, to them gave *He* power to become the sons of God, even to them that believe *on His name*" (John 1:12). It was Peter who said, "According as His divine power hath given unto us all things that pertain unto life and godliness, through the knowledge of *Him* . . ." (2 Peter 1:3). Paul taught that God has blessed us with all spiritual blessings ". . . *in Christ*" (Ephesians 1:3), and he prayed that the Christians might be illuminated and grow, " . . . in the knowledge of *Him*" (Ephesians 1:17). Of his own spiritual life Paul said, " . . . *Christ* liveth in me . . ." (Galatians 2:20); "For to me to live is *Christ* . . ." (Philippians 1:21); and "That I may know *Him* . . ." (Philippians 3:10).

The identical message is proclaimed in the doctrinal explanation of Christianity. Jesus Christ is the object of faith (Acts 16:31); the source of all wisdom and knowledge (Colossians 2:3); the Savior of mankind (1 John 4:14); the Head of the Church (Ephesians 1:22); the believer's peace (Ephesians 2:14); his wisdom, righteousness, sanctification and redemption (1 Corinthians 1:30); his power (1 Corinthians 1:24); and the One in whom all believers are complete (Colossians 2:10).

Christianity is surely a belief, a group of doctrines, a relationship, an ethic, a way of life, a form of service, a living hope, a demanding imperative, and a transforming deliverance, but all of these are rooted in and revolve around the Person of Jesus Christ the Son of God. Christianity is first of all Jesus Christ.

## A SERIOUS WARNING:
## Christianity is Often Perverted.

Religious perversions are not produced by agnostics or atheists but by well-meaning Christians. In the attempt to cure some failure in practice, one facet of Biblical Christianity has often been overemphasized. When this facet is made the central factor in Christianity, a perversion results. There are at least four common perversions taught in the church today.

(1) One of the most common perversions is the misconception that Christianity revolves around the church. Though even a casual reading of the New Testament will indicate the importance of this divine institution, God did not bring the church into existence to be the center of our lives. That place must be reserved for and filled by Jesus Christ, the Head of the Church. There are many today who have given the place of Christ to the church. In misplaced zeal these have taken that which is secondary and made it first.

When the church is made the central factor in Christianity it is utilized in at least three ways. The church is used as a source of spirituality, as the means whereby spirituality is maintained, and as the basis of measuring spirituality. In reply to the question, "How can I become a spiritual person and then maintain my spirituality?" the answer is given, "Attend church regularly."

Spirituality is not the automatic by-product of church attendance. Nor is it, in itself, the measuring rod for distinguishing between those who are spiritual and those who are not. The church has its divinely ordained place of importance. It is not, however, a panacea. One may be constantly in church and yet miss Him who is the Head of the Church.

(2) A second popular perversion of Christianity is legalism. In this zealous misinterpretation of the Bible, rules are placed at the center of Christianity and all must revolve around certain practices of life. The "don'ts" of this type of "Christian" life receive undue emphasis. The Christian is one who has stopped doing certain things!

The key to spirituality, for this way of thinking, is the wholehearted acceptance of certain rules as absolutes. Obedience to these rules is a guarantee as well as the mark of spirituality.

There is no question about the emphasis of the Bible upon obedience. And there are many commandments in the Scripture which the Christian must obey. However, these commandments are not an end in themselves. They have been given to us as the *means* whereby we obey God. The Christian is not to obey the commandment alone. He is to *obey God*—by keeping the commandment. This is the reason why love and obedience are inseparably related in the Bible (John 14: 15, 21, 23; 15:10; 1 John 2:5; 5:3; 2 John 6).

The legalist is almost never content to stop with the commandments of the Scripture. New rules must be invented which are somehow twisted into becoming the application of Biblical principles. God, love, and personal freedom are soon eclipsed. It is frightfully easy to obey all the rules of the legalist and even the commandments of the Bible and yet not give first place to one's Lord.

(3) A third perversion of Christianity may be called emotionalism or the overemphasis on religious experience. A certain type of experience may be proclaimed as the secret of spirituality and as the distinguishing mark of spiritual people. In this way a personal subjective authority is substituted for the authority of divine revelation. To have an inner feeling of spirituality and to be able to produce at will some manifestation of religious zeal may be a great comfort to some people but it is not described in the Bible as being of the essence of Christianity.

Religious experiences and emotional feelings are surely a part of Biblical Christianity. These, however, are the *results* and not the causes of the work of grace. A person is not necessarily right with God simply because his emotion so testifies. Non-Christians have been known to produce elaborate and sustained religious experiences.

When Christianity is made to revolve around emotionalism or religious experience, and not around the Person of Jesus Christ, there is the ever present danger of shifting the standard of authority from God and His revelation to ourselves and our experiences. One may be so preoccupied with his experience that he may bypass Christ, the believer's sanctification (1 Corinthians 1:30).

(4) A fourth illustration of how Christianity may suffer from perversion is the over-emphasis on Christian service. A certain type or

types of service may be placed at the center of Christianity. Here Christian service becomes the source of spirituality and the manner whereby it is maintained. The spiritual people are those who perform a stereotyped service which usually revolves around the church.

There is no question but that the Scriptures pronounce a commission over every Christian. To be a Christian is to be a worker. However, what was said above about obeying God may be said here. Christian service is not an end in itself. This is only one way whereby God is loved, worshipped and obeyed—in practice. It is all too easy to be intensely engaged in service and yet not be serving God. Many times it is the church which is being served, or the pastor, or even our own conscience.

Christianity does not revolve around a form of service; it revolves around the Person of Jesus Christ. It is possible to be taken up with a great variety of Christian services and yet not be committed to the Lord of the harvest field.

As Christians we must take a very firm stand against ourselves and against the perversions of Christianity. It is easy but sinful to transfer our love and devotion from God to something associated with God. When this happens we are more in love with religion than with God! Only He may be the object of our affection.

When you have mastered this lesson, answer the questions in Exam 1 and mail the exam for correction.

7

# HIGHER GROUND

Exam
Grade_____

Name_____
                    (print plainly)

Address _____

                              Zip          Class
City_____State _____ Code _____ Number _____

Instructor _____

## LESSON 1

*In the blank space in the right-hand margin write the letter of the correct answer.*

1.  The basic essential for living the Christian life is
    a. the desire to live it
    b. the desire to live it and the knowledge of the
       principles which govern it
    c. willingness to accept defeat philosophically
    d. membership in a Bible-teaching church                 _____

2.  The great bedrock underlying true Christianity is
    a. an attractive ethic
    b. a moral code
    c. dynamic psychology
    d. an authoritative revelation                           _____

3.  Which of the following best expresses the rule for belief and
    practice in the Christian life? Christianity
    a. is highly plastic in character and can be molded to suit any
       culture, temperament or situation
    b. is based on certain basic truths which can and should be
       interpreted according to the presuppositions of the inter-
       preter
    c. must rest upon the Bible and no one must tamper with
       its content, meaning or authority
    d. is subjective and its ultimate court of appeal is the exper-
       ience of the individual or the corporate experience of the
       group                                                 _____

4. As a Christian, the place at which to start in putting to the test one's beliefs and practices is with
   a. an ecstatic experience
   b. the historical Christ made known in the Bible
   c. a thorough examination of the doctrines of the church
   d. a study of comparative religion    _____

5. The Lord Jesus insisted that Christianity
   a. is a matter of keeping the law of Moses on a high, spiritual plane
   b. involves a personal relationship with Himself
   c. is a noble ideal but conceded that such precepts as those found in the Sermon on the Mount are beyond the possibility of daily practice under normal conditions
   d. is largely a matter of code and creed, rite and ritual    _____

6. A person becomes a child of God by
   a. joining the church
   b. being baptized and taking communion
   c. being good and helping others
   d. fanning the "divine spark" into flame
   e. believing on the Lord Jesus and receiving Him into the life
   f. all the above methods    _____

7. "The way to maintain spirituality is to attend church regularly." Such a statement
   a. shows a misunderstanding of the nature and purpose of the church
   b. expresses the basic truth that dynamic Christian living is necessarily linked with constant Christian fellowship
   c. gives the church the place God intends it to have in the believer's life
   d. deliberately, willfully and unpardonably perverts the truth    _____

8. The legalist is
   a. right because rules belong at the very heart of Christianity
   b. wrong because the New Testament lays down no rules for living the Christian life
   c. right because God insists on obedience
   d. wrong because legalism results in a negative kind of Christianity foreign to the New Testament    _____

**9.** Religious feelings and emotional experiences are
   a. part of Christianity, but are the results, not the basis of it
   b. entirely foreign to New Testament Christianity
   c. the sole evidence that one is in the will of God
   d. native to Christianity and foreign to other religions _____

**10.** Christian service
   a. is what Christianity is all about for "to be a Christian is to be a worker"
   b. may be a snare for it is possible to be serving something or someone else and neglecting God
   c. should be neglected since it can all too easily become a snare
   d. is an acceptable substitute for personal devotion to the Lord Jesus Christ _____

## WHAT DO YOU SAY?

Have you been snared by any of the misconceptions discussed in this lesson? If so, what do you think now?

_____

_____

_____

_____

_____

*MAIL TO address shown on back outside cover.*
*PLEASE enclose a stamped addressed envelope for the return of your corrected exam.*

# The Nature of Biblical Christianity (Cont.)

## THE BIBLICAL DESCRIPTION:
### Christ-Centered Christianity is Final Authority.

Christianity is not an institution, not a list of rules, not a religious experience, and not a certain type of service. Christianity revolves around a Person, Jesus Christ the Son of God.

When one asks, "What does this mean in practice?" the Biblical answer is "final authority."

The engineer and the physicist are inescapably and rigidly limited by the laws of nature. They will succeed only by careful working in harmony with these laws. They are under an authority which is external to them and over which they have no control. The engineer may have an intense dislike for concrete. But this personal dislike does not give him license to build the bridge out of pápier maché.

And so it is in Christianity. God has revealed Himself. This revelation is no less authoritative than the laws of physics. It is, in fact, much more so. The Scripture is emphatically clear on the necessity of repentance, the new birth, faith, love, confession of sin, and obedience. In these areas the right and the wrong has been clearly stated. The Christian may not live as though God has not spoken, as though Jesus Christ has not come, as though the crucifixion and the resurrection did not happen, as though the Bible were not written.

It would be ridiculous for the airplane builder to think that he could operate successfully without taking into account the laws of gravity. It would be even more so for the Christian to believe that he could succeed without a wholehearted acceptance of the authority of divine revelation.

Such an acceptance is exceedingly difficult to make. To do so is to shift the source of authority from ourselves to God. As sinful persons we unconsciously attribute final authority to ourselves. We soon learn that we are not intuitive experts in the areas of chemistry, architecture, thermodynamics or similar fields. But every one of us, by nature, believes he is an absolute expert in the truths of religion.

There are at least three wrong responses which we make to the revelation of God. We reject it, we resist it, and we pervert it. Even in the life of the committed Christian these three may be present at one time. Although such an individual may submit to divine authority in many areas of daily life, he will, in some areas, reject the will of God, perhaps almost unconsciously so; in others he will accept it partially, with resistance; and in other areas he will attempt to succeed with a perversion of divine revelation.

Such a sinful response is intensified in the life of the non-Christian. It is not unusual for such a person to glibly call God "a liar" (1 John 5:10). In the Scriptures God has said that all men are unrighteous and sinners (Romans 3:10, 23), but the non-Christian states, "I'm not a sinner!" God has said that no man may come to Him except through Jesus Christ (John 14:6) and by the avenue of the new birth (John 3:3, 5), but the non-Christian affirms, "I don't need to believe in anyone but myself and I'll get there by my good works!"

There is only one correct response to divine authority. It is that of total acceptance. In the inner spiritual life it means complete surrender. In the manifestation of spiritual life it means complete obedience. It is surrender and obedience to a Person.

## THE SCRIPTURAL FOUNDATION:
### Jesus Christ, His Work, and His Word.

God is final authority. And in Christianity we are dealing with God, not with a man, an institution, an experience, a way of thinking, or even a way of life.

The authority in Christianity is reflected in its three foundation stones. These form the minimal content of the gospel. The Apostle Paul stated that the gospel had to do with (1) Jesus Christ, (2) His death, burial, and resurrection, and (3) the Scriptures (1 Corinthians 15:1-4). The same threefold emphasis is found in the post-resurrection instruction of our Lord (Luke 24:44-48).

The authority of God is vested first of all in Jesus Christ. He is, according to the Scriptures, the eternal Son of God. Out of love He became a member of the human race to be man's Redeemer.

The Lord Jesus Christ declared that He was the truth (John 14:6) and the Apostle Paul stated that all wisdom and knowledge finds its source in Him (Colossians 2:3). The authority of God therefore rests in a Person. We may not "refuse . . . Him that speaketh" (Hebrews 12:25). Without Him we can do nothing (John 15:5).

Genuine Christianity is a manifestation of God in human history. The nature, characteristics and structure of Christianity has been determined by who and what God is. God is holy. We have been commanded to be holy (1 Peter 1:15, 16). God is love. We have been commanded to love one another as we have been loved (John 13:34). The list is quite endless. God has revealed *Himself.* When this revelation is correctly practiced, the result is Biblical Christianity.

The authority in Christianity is also found in the redemptive work of the Lord Jesus. His work may be described as the deeds of God in history. These deeds determine the structure of Christianity.

An illustration of this is found in the Old Testament. There we are told how God supernaturally delivered His people through the events described as the Exodus. This deed of God formed the basis as well as the structure of the Theocracy. The Hebrew people were therefore a redeemed race. They belonged to God. The yearly memorial of the Passover was given to remind them of these truths. The very roots of their nation, their calling, and their religion were found in the Exodus.

Biblical Christianity has been unalterably structured by the incarnation of Jesus Christ, from His life and ministry, from His crucifixion, His resurrection, the ascension and from Pentecost. When the Christian sins, acting as though he belonged to himself, he is acting out of

**15**

harmony with the character and deeds of God. Sin is therefore described in the Bible as "lawlessness" (1 John 3:4, A.S.V.). This is to emphasize that it is a violation or contradiction of authority. To sin against God is to act contrary to His nature and contrary to the deeds of God in history.

Since the authority in Biblical Christianity is found in the work of Christ, it is necessary for the Christian to accept the evaluation and the demands of these deeds. Christ died to deliver us from the guilt and power of sin. The only correct response we may make is to accept this evaluation of sin. Man is under a solemn authority to repent of sin, to condemn and forsake it in all of its forms, to receive the forgiveness of salvation and the daily deliverance and enablement provided by Jesus Christ for a successful Christian life. The Christian may not live as though Christ did not die and rise from the grave. These deeds have authoritatively structured every facet of Biblical Christianity.

The authority in and for Christianity is also found in the Holy Scripture. This does not mean that the Scripture is a third type of authority. The three foundation stones of Christianity, the Person of Jesus Christ, His deeds in history, and His Word, are inseparably related. God has not only revealed Himself in history but also through the inspired record and interpretation of His work. What we know of God and His work is through His authoritative Word.

When Jesus Christ was on earth He referred to and utilized the Scripture as final authority. He spoke of it as "the commandment of God," and as "the Word of God" (Mark 7:6-13). Of His opponents He repeatedly asked, " . . . have ye not read . . .?" (Matthew 12:3, 5; 19:4). He quoted the Scriptures in His temptation (Matthew 4:4, 7, 10) and reminded the disciples that all which had been prophesied of Him would surely come to pass (Luke 18:31).

The Lord Jesus pointed out that it was contradictory indeed to call Him "Lord" and then disobey His Word (Luke 6:46). In harmony with this the Bible teaches the inseparable relationship of love for God and obedience to His Word (John 14:15, 23, 24; 1 John 2:3-5; 5:3; 2 John 6). We may not presume that our actions are acceptable with God or that we are expressing love to God while disobeying the

Scripture. Such an attitude is a violation of the very structure of Christianity.

Christ-centered Christianity comes to us as final authority. It is a manifestation of God's character which, in turn, has been revealed through the deeds of God in history, and in His inspired Word.

## THE INESCAPABLE RESULTS:
### Spiritual Freedom or Slavery.

It is not enough to live in harmony with the church, to obey all the rules of the legalist, to perform all the ceremonies of the liturgist, to say all the right words of the Pharisee, to have the right experiences of the emotionalist, and to perform the right services of the Christian worker. We *may* do all these things without commitment, without faith and love, and without serious question as to whether God were dead or alive. We may, indeed, do all these things and be lost.

Christianity demands a complete surrender of one's self to God in the acceptance of His authority. This surrender is a personal subjugation of one's will to Another. The Apostle Paul described himself as " . . . a slave of Jesus Christ" (Romans 1:1).

Christianity has been designed by God to be operative. Therefore, it must be put into practice before it becomes effective. It is the provision of a *daily* redemption. When we are in total subjection to God and live in daily obedience, the power and grace of Biblical Christianity will flow into our life.

Since more will be said about this later it may be sufficient here to point out the Biblical nature of this principle. Simply stated it is this: *when we obey, God works.* This is in no way meant to deny the sovereignty of God nor the depravity of man. All faith and obedience can only be traced back to God's sovereign generosity.

The promise of Jesus Christ is simple and clear. He said, "And ye shall know the truth, and the truth shall make you free" (John 8: 32). The word "know" in Scripture designates more than a mere intellectual apprehension. It includes decisions of faith and correct practice. It is self evident from the Scripture and from what has been said before that to "know the truth" is the practice of a personal relationship.

The freedom promised by Christ is primarily spiritual. It is the freedom of the inner man. It is freedom to be the right kind of person. To be able to choose your own thoughts and actions without being pressured by men, circumstances, or sinful desires. It is the freedom produced by the grace and power of God which enables one to know right and wrong, to practice the right, and to enjoy it.

The warning of Jesus Christ is equally clear. He said, " . . . whosoever committeth sin is the servant of sin" (John 8:34). To "commit sin" is the opposite of "knowing the truth." It is the rejection of the personal authority of Christ-centered Christianity and the elevation of self to the position of God. It is the practice of making one's self the final authority, and personal satisfaction the goal of one's endeavor. When this choice is made and practiced it produces slavery. One becomes enslaved to one's self. Instead of all things revolving around Jesus Christ, they revolve around one's self. Freedom has been lost, selfishness is practiced, and any enjoyment is highly temporary.

The choice is ours and the results are inescapable—freedom or slavery.

When you have mastered this lesson, take the first part of Exam 2 (covering lesson 2), questions 1-10 on pages 27-29 (right after lesson 3). Remember, you will not turn this exam in for correction until after you have done lesson 3.

# The Characteristics of Biblical Christianity

## CHRISTIANITY IS HISTORICAL:
### It is not a myth or legend.

The incarnation of Jesus Christ may not be classed with the mythical birth of Athena who sprang forth fully armed from the head of her father Zeus. The events of the Bible *really happened*. They are historical events!

Christianity traces its source to the revelation of God in history. This revelation cannot be separated from the incarnation of Jesus Christ, His miracles, and in particular His resurrection. We have seen that these deeds are not only the basis but also determine the structure of Biblical Christianity. If these deeds did not happen historically, then Christianity must be thoroughly and completely rejected.

We are left with no alternative. The Scriptures are adamant in their demand. This is particularly true of the physical resurrection of Jesus Christ. The resurrection is a part of the ministry of Christ from its very beginning to its end (John 2:18-21; Matthew 20:17-19). When He was pressed to give a sign, He spoke of His resurrection (Matthew 12:38-40). The same is true in the confession of His deity (Matthew 16:13-21; Mark 8:27-31; Luke 9:18-22).

Even the most rudimentary listing of the importance of the resurrection is overwhelming. The Scriptures frankly state that the resurrection affirms the deity of Jesus Christ (Romans 1:4); that it is an important evidence for the truthfulness of the gospel (Acts 17:31); that it is an indispensable part of the content of the gospel (Acts 4:2; 17:18; 1 Corinthians 15:1-4, 13-19); that the divine provision of salvation is found in the resurrection (1 Peter 1:3; Romans 4:25); that a confession of belief in the resurrection is a necessity for salvation (Romans 10:9, 10); that it is the source of the believer's hope of his own resurrection (1 Corinthians 15:20); that it is the provision of grace and power for the Christian life (Romans 6:5-14; Philippians 3:10); and that it was the message of the early Church (Acts 1:22; 2:22-36; 3:12-19; 5:29-32; 10:34-43; 13:26-41).

## CHRISTIANITY IS SUPERNATURAL:
### It is not a result of human desire or natural law.

Christianity has not been produced by a wish-fulfilling compulsion of an insecure race. The eternal and infinite God has revealed Himself within the realms of time and space. His activity, therefore, cannot be explained by utilization of natural law. Christianity has within it the element of the miraculous.

This characteristic is an affirmation that God has an existence independent of and separate from His creation. This rejects the view that God and the universe are the same, as held by pantheism, or that God has withdrawn Himself from His creation, as taught by deism.

The supernatural origin of Christianity may be illustrated in the birth and nature of the Jewish religion. Both sacred and secular history testify that Israel worshipped one God (monotheism) when the surrounding nations were worshipping many gods (polytheism). She worshipped a sovereign God, who ruled over all, while her neighbors worshipped gods related to certain sections of land. Her religion was ethically and religiously moral while the religions about Palestine were tainted with immorality. To explain these fundamental differences is very difficult on a naturalistic basis. It is hardly sufficient to refer to Jewish genes and chromosomes.

## CHRISTIANITY IS REDEMPTIVE:
### It is not mere religious advice.

Christianity purports to be practical and powerfully so. Its leading exponent, the Apostle Paul, stated that he was not ashamed of the gospel because it worked (Romans 1:16)! This is why the term "gospel" has generally been designated as "good news."

God has provided in Jesus Christ and His sacrificial death a spiritual deliverance. He has provided life (Ephesians 2:5) for our death (Ephesians 2:1); forgiveness (Colossians 2:13) for our guilt (Romans 3:23); righteousness (Romans 8:3, 4) for our unrighteousness (Romans 3:10); reconciliation (Ephesians 2:13-16) for our alienation (Ephesians 2:12); and cleansing (1 Corinthians 6:11) for our depravity (1 Corinthians 6:9, 10). The list is endless. Why one would reject Christianity, when there is so much of practical good to be obtained, is beyond human logic. It is, in fact, diabolical.

In the Scripture the redemptive characteristic of Christianity is portrayed by such words as "grace" and "power." The former generally indicates the work of Jesus Christ whereby man may be freely accepted by God (John 1:17; Ephesians 2:8, 9). The latter usually designates the provision or the effect of God's grace (1 Corinthians 1:24; Ephesians 1:19-23).

Christianity is redemptive because there is a Redeemer. Jesus Christ, the Son of God, fulfilled God's demand in that He bore man's judgment on Calvary (Romans 5:6-11; 2 Corinthians 5:21; 1 Peter 2:24). What we deserve—fell upon Him. We have been redeemed.

## CHRISTIANITY IS REPRESENTATIVE:
### It is more than a religious philosophy.

When Jesus Christ became a member of the human race, He did so as man's representative. In His baptism He identified Himself with the human race. In His temptation, as Representative Man, the Last Adam, He met and mastered Satan. In a sense all believers were represented in that triumph (John 17:2, 9, 19).

21

The work of men who have been given the legal right of representation may illustrate this facet of Christianity. Such men may travel to a distant city or country. As the representative of some firm or institution they may sign their name to a great sheaf of orders. In a legal sense the president of the firm is signing his name in his representative capacity. So are the vice-presidents and all who may be involved. What their representative does involves all of them.

And so it is in the work of Jesus Christ. He lived His righteous life in fulfillment of God's demand (Romans 8:3) and that life becomes my life when I believe (Romans 8:4). He died, and that death was the crowning act of a life of obedience. In that death I am made righteous. It was a representative death (Romans 5:19; 2 Corinthians 5:21). He died *for* me (1 Corinthians 15:3) and, in a representative sense, He died *as* me. Christ not only died for the believer, the believer died in and with Him (Romans 6:1-8; Galatians 2:20). He was resurrected in and with Christ, he has ascended in and with Christ and is now seated "in the heavenlies" (Ephesians 2:5, 6; Colossians 3:1-3).

The practical application of this characteristic of Christianity is breath-taking. All the value of the representative work of Jesus Christ has been given to the believer! It has been imputed to him as a free gift. It has been written into his spiritual bank account. This is why the Apostle Paul stated that the believer, in Christ, has been blessed with all spiritual blessings (Ephesians 1:3), " . . . all things are your's" (1 Corinthians 3:21).

## CHRISTIANITY IS PERSONAL:
**It is not theoretical or abstract.**

It is Jesus Christ who stands at the door (Revelation 3:20). He bids no one stand at arms-length.

Christianity not only revolves around Jesus Christ, He is *Himself* the divine provision for all of man's redemptive needs.

In salvation man receives, through repentance and faith, the Person of Jesus Christ, who becomes his Savior (John 1:12; Acts 16:31). Salvation is therefore, not so much an experience, as it is a relationship with the Son of God.

The same principle holds true in all facets of the Christian life. The Apostle Paul described the Lord Jesus as the believer's "wisdom," "power," "righteousness," "sanctification," and "redemption" (1 Corinthians 1:24, 30). All areas of man's need can be subsumed under these five headings. God has made Himself available to us in and through the Person and work of Jesus Christ.

In harmony with this truth Paul sought to "know Him" (Philippians 3:10); and emphasized the importance of being conformed to His image (Romans 8:28, 29). He spoke of Christ's presence in the believer as "the hope of glory" (Colossians 1:27), and prayed that the saints at Ephesus might grow in their "knowledge of Him" (Ephesians 1:17).

The invitation is clear, "Come unto Me . . . I will give you rest" (Matthew 11:28).

## CHRISTIANITY IS REVELATORY:
**It is not an ambiguous guess.**

God is not an object which man may subject to his own scrutiny. If God had not chosen to reveal Himself, man would have been left in a religious enigma.

That God would make Himself known is beyond man's wildest dream. But it is true.

## CHRISTIANITY IS AUTHORITATIVE:
**It is not a compilation of subjective human opinion.**

That God has spoken is an inescapable fact. How to assess such a "speaking" is insurmountably difficult. The word "authoritative" is indeed necessary but woefully weak. No word or concept is adequate here.

The extent of man's depravity is portrayed in his arrogant "ability" to hear and yet reject the revelation of God as irrelevant or even as false and to disobey God with impudent smugness!

## CHRISTIANITY IS COVENANTAL:
**It is not a powerless invitation of dubious promise.**

The invitation of salvation and its attendant promises comes to us with power from on high. It is accompanied with a life-giving power (John 5:24, 25; Ephesians 2:1, 6; Colossians 2:13; 1 Peter 1:3).

As a result, the true believer is brought into a covenantal relationship with God. This is the manifestation of the Father's covenant or promise with the Son in the covenant of redemption (John 17:2, 4, 6-12, 22-26) which was made before time began. The "new covenant" of this present time (Hebrews 8:6-13; 9:15) was anticipated in the Old Testament covenant (Jeremiah 31:31-37). Jesus Christ is the Mediator of the new covenant (Hebrews 8:6) and the believer's Surety (Hebrews 7:22), so that all the salvation provisions of the new covenant will surely be his (Hebrews 8:10-13). The new covenant was initiated or ratified by the work of Jesus Christ in His atonement (Matthew 26:26-28; Hebrews 7:11-28; 9:15-28; 10:1-24). One of the purposes in the ordinance of the Lord's Supper is to remind the believer of his covenantal relationship with God (1 Corinthians 11:23-26).

The true Christian does not belong to himself; he belongs to God. Through the vicarious work of Jesus Christ and the application of this work in divine sovereignty, God has brought the Christian into an eternal covenantal relationship with Himself.


## CHRISTIANITY IS EXCLUSIVE:
**It is not merely the highest form of the human religious quest.**

Christianity is the result of *divine* revelation. It is a disclosure by God, not a discovery by man.

There is only one way to God. Jesus Christ said, "I am the way, . . . no man cometh unto the Father, but by Me" (John 14:6).

Christianity is not the most highly developed form of man's search for God. It is not related to such religions as Animism and Hinduism as the fruit and flower are related to the seed. Christianity has not been produced by a religious evolutionary force.

While there are elements of truth in all the religions, Christianity stands alone as the truth.

Christianity, we have seen, revolves around the Person of Jesus Christ. Every religion, therefore, which does not believe in Jesus Christ as the eternal Son of God and practice His Word can only be condemned as false (Matthew 7:21-29; John 3:36; 8:24; Romans 10:9, 10; 1 John 4:1-6; 5:9-13).

To be acceptable with God one must be more than sincere. He must be both sincere and right (John 4:24)!


## CHRISTIANITY IS DEMANDING:
### It is not a weak, sentimental, permissive avocation.

" . . . Give up yourself . . . Surrender your rights . . . Lose your life . . . Follow Me! then." Such statements break through all attempts to treat Christianity as a tolerant hobby. They summarize Christ's demands for discipleship (Mark 8:34, 35).

The mandate within Biblical Christianity is not found primarily in its commandments. It is found in the One around whom all in Christianity revolves—Jesus Christ—and in His love.

To be loved by God is the most demanding, obligatory, inescapable imperative that could ever be conceived. To be so loved means to be recognized as a person by the Creator. It means to be the recipient, in some way, of the evidence of God's love—the giving of His Son (John 3:16; 1 John 3:16; 4:8-21).

That God would love and give Himself in a voluntary sacrifice brings to all men an unavoidable and all-inclusive demand. It is that we love and give up ourselves to God. It means to recognize Him for who He is and to give Him His rightful place in our lives.

To give up a sin here or there, to relinquish a pleasure, to give money, talent, time, and even one's complete life is quite irrelevant (1 Corinthians 13). God wants and demands the *person*. He wants you, your heart—not your money or your platitudes (Proverbs 3:1, 5, 6; 4:4, 23; 23-26; Matthew 22:37, 38). Once the heart is given, then the commandments find their rightful place. They become the means whereby one's love for God is expressed in daily life (John 14:15, 21, 23; 1 John 2:5; 5:3; 2 John 6).


## CHRISTIANITY IS CONTEMPORANEOUS:
### It is not a specimen of an antique religious practice.

Christianity is historical but it may never be relegated to the historical past. The Christian may not worship a first century God. The true and living God is the great " . . . I am" (John 8:58). He is the same today (Hebrews 13:8) and is ever present with His own (Matthew 28:20). God is not bound by time and space.

There is something extremely wrong in asking for "the old time religion," and "the old time power." God has nothing "old" to give. He who is the truth, with His life, forgiveness, deliverance, authority, demands, and power, is always in the present tense (Hebrews 3:7, 13; 13:8).

When you are ready, complete Exam 2 by answering questions 11-20 on pages 29-31. (You should have already answered questions 1-10 as part of your study of lesson 2.)

When you have answered all the questions in Exam 2, mail the exam for correction.

# HIGHER GROUND

Exam

Name_____Grade_____
(print plainly)

Address _____

|  | | Zip | Class |

City_____ State _____ Code _____ Number _____

Instructor _____

## LESSON 2

*In the blank space in the right-hand margin write the letter of the correct answer.*

1. The final authority of the Lord Jesus
   a. is a fundamentalist myth since all things are relative
   b. was unknown in primitive Christianity and is a Pauline concept superimposed upon the original concept of Jesus of Nazareth
   c. is not so final after all when we look at the way it is defied
   d. translates into practical terms the fact that "Christianity is Christ"               _____

2. On such matters as the new birth, repentance, faith, love, sin, etc., the Bible
   a. gives an uncertain sound since it has a different set of rules in the New Testament than those which appear in the Old Testament
   b. is very largely silent
   c. is adamant and unyielding
   d. speaks with unreasonable dogmatism totally unacceptable today               _____

3. Sometimes even the committed Christian will find himself
   a. rejecting parts of the Bible
   b. resisting parts of the Bible
   c. perverting parts of the Bible
   d. doing all of the above
   e. doing none of the above               _____

27

4. When a non-Christian says that he is "doing his best" and that he expects to get to heaven by his good works he is
   a. in effect calling God a liar
   b. expressing a commendable belief in himself
   c. in step with the spirit of the Bible which encourages good works
   d. voicing a popular religious sentiment which must have much to commend it since it is so popular and universally accepted

5. Which of the following is *NOT* one of the fundamental corner stones of Christianity?
   a. The Scriptures
   b. The Church
   c. The Person of Christ
   d. The death, burial and resurrection of Christ

6. In John 14:6 the Lord Jesus declared Himself to be "the way, the truth and the life" and that
   a. He ever lives to act as Mediator for those who would come to God by Him
   b. it is impossible to come to God except by Him
   c. he who would come to God must believe that He is and that He is the Rewarder of all those who diligently seek Him
   d. when we know the truth the truth will set us free

7. Sin is described in the Bible as
   a. "lawlessness"—because when a person sins he is behaving as though God had no claim upon him
   b. "an error of mortal mind"—since sin only exists in the mind and imagination
   c. "weakness"—because it results from the imperfection of the human will
   d. "sickness"—because it can be cured with proper psychological and religious therapy

8. Which of the following are inseparable?
   a. What God is and what we are therefore to be
   b. The Person of Christ, His deeds in history and His Word
   c. A love for God and an obedience to His Word
   d. All the above

9. The power and grace of Biblical Christianity flows into our lives only when we
   a. yield and obey
   b. try hard enough to make Christianity work
   c. give mental assent to divine truth
   d. fully understand the Bible _____

10. The freedom promised by the Lord Jesus Christ is freedom from
    a. want
    b. temptation
    c. sin
    d. suffering _____

## WHAT DO YOU SAY?

To what extent do you detect in your own life a tendency to rationalize clear commands of God which run counter to your own desires and inclinations?

_____

_____

_____

_____

_____

## LESSON 3

*In the blank space in the right-hand margin write the letter of the correct answer.*

11. The virgin birth of Christ as narrated in the New Testament and the story of Athena
    a. have much in common because both are based on actual historical incidents
    b. have this in common that both are myths
    c. have much in common because both are interesting religious notions only the one is Hebrew in origin and the other Greek
    d. have nothing in common: the virgin birth of Christ actually happened; the birth of Athena is mythical _____

**12.** The resurrection of Christ must be regarded as
   a. an actual event which took place in history
   b. an inspiring religious idea having its roots in the Egyptian Osiris myth
   c. a later addition to Christianity added to the purer concepts of Christ by the Church Fathers
   d. a minor doctrine of Christian belief, faith in which is optional

—————

**13.** Where do we read in the New Testament that the resurrection of Christ is essential to salvation? In
   a. Romans 4:25
   b. Romans 10:9, 10
   c. 1 Corinthians 15:13-19
   d. all the above passages
   e. none of the above passages

—————

**14.** Which of the following best describes Christianity? It is
   a. a non-supernatural faith evolved by mankind to meet a real spiritual need of the race
   b. supernatural in as much as God has revealed Himself in terms of time and space
   c. a truly cosmic faith for it identifies God with the universe in a thoroughly pantheistic way
   d. the only faith which gives hope to mankind in a universe from which God has withdrawn Himself so completely that theologians can state that He is dead

—————

**15.** Paul was able to unblushingly proclaim the gospel because
   a. it made no demands upon him to believe in miracles as did the Judaism he rejected and in which he was trained
   b. he knew from personal experience the power of it in his own life and in the lives of others
   c. it appealed to the Jewish passion for *light;* to the Greek passion for *logic;* and to the Roman passion for *law*
   d. he was an impractical idealist who was fascinated by the subtler points of Christian theology and by the finer points of its ethic

—————

**16.** When the Bible speaks of "grace" it generally has in mind
a. the poise, charm and dynamism which make most Christians so attractive to their non-Christian acquaintances
b. a form of prayer normally said before meals by devout believers
c. the condition of soul imparted by the sacraments of the church
d. the work of Christ which makes us acceptable to God apart from any effort of our own _____

**17.** The New Testament sees the whole human race headed up in two representative men. These men are
a. Moses and Elijah
b. Moses and Christ
c. Adam and Christ
d. David and Solomon
e. Abraham and David _____

**18.** Which of the following is true?
a. Christ as my Redeemer died *for* me
b. Christ as my Representative died *as* me.
c. Christ as my Savior lives *in* me
d. All the above are true _____

**19.** God's relationship with the believer in the Lord Jesus is essentially
a. conditional because it depends on the ability of the believer to "keep it up"
b. contractual because it links God and the believer in a covenant relationship
c. confessional because failure to confess Christ day by day results in its termination
d. congregational because it can only be maintained in constant fellowship with other believers _____

**20.** The demands God makes upon us as believers are
a. unrealistic in view of the many other demands (home, business, pleasure, friends, etc.) which are made upon us
b. easy, limited and secondary in character allowing us to live as we please in this life and yet be assured of heaven hereafter
c. total and mandatory and arise out of the very nature of our redemption
d. of such a nature that, in the last analysis, we are saved by our own good works _____

## WHAT DO YOU SAY?

Which of the characteristics of Biblical Christianity discussed in this lesson most challenges you?

_____

_____

_____

_____

_____

*MAIL TO address shown on back outside cover.*
*PLEASE enclose a stamped addressed envelope for the return of your corrected exam.*

# The Application of Biblical Christianity

**THE IMPORTANT QUESTION:**
**"How is the Christian Related to God?"**

Christianity, we have seen, revolves around the Person of Jesus Christ. We are not told in the Scripture to believe on the church, nor in our good works, nor in baptism or the Lord's Supper. We are to believe in Jesus Christ.

Because of who Jesus Christ is and because of what He has done for us in His death, we are commanded to repent of our sins and to believe in Him as our Lord and Savior (Luke 13:3; 24:46, 47; Acts 26:20; Romans 10:9, 10; 1 John 3:23). This is the most important decision one may make. Without it one is still under the condemnation of God (John 3:18, 36); he will be rejected by Christ (Matthew 7:21-29; John 8:24); and be eternally lost (Revelation 20:11-15).

"Believe on the Lord Jesus Christ, and thou shalt be saved . . ." is the promise of God (Acts 16:31).

When we obey God and believe on Jesus Christ as Lord and Savior then the Scripture describes our condition by such words as "saved," "adoption," "begotten," "redeemed," "forgiven," and "justified" (Ephesians 2:8; 1:5; 1 Peter 1:3, 18; Colossians 2:13; Romans 5:1).

Such words signify a *standing* before God. They indicate a spiritual position, a relationship which has been obtained for the believer by Jesus Christ through His death. The believer is seen as having received the benefits of the work of Jesus Christ. The value of Christ's work has been imputed to him and he is therefore "saved," "adopted," "begotten," etc., and brought into the relationship of salvation (Romans 5:1-11; 8:31-39; Ephesians 1:3-14; Colossians 2:10-15; 1 Peter 1:1-5; 1 John 5:9-13).

The Scripture describes all believers, therefore, as "complete" (Colossians 2:10). In the Greek, in which the New Testament was written, this word means "possess fully" and the grammatical construction indicated a finished product.

To explain what he meant in calling the Christian "complete" the Apostle Paul indicated that the believer in Jesus Christ "fully possessed" at least five things.

He has received a *spiritual cleansing* (Colossians 2:11). This means that the moral uncleanness which characterizes every non-believer (Isaiah 64:6), has been washed away. The believer, even though he may feel unclean, has been cleansed (1 Corinthians 6:11).

The Christian, as "complete," has been *"quickened"* by God (Colossians 2:13a). The word "quickened" means "to make alive." This teaches the great truth that God has given eternal life to all who believe on His Son (John 3:16, 36; 1 John 5:11, 12). Though once dead to God (Ephesians 2:1), the believer now possesses life (John 10:28) and has experienced the new birth (John 3:3, 5).

The third possession of the Christian is *forgiveness* (Colossians 2:13b). The Bible, by use of the word "all" emphasizes the universality of this forgiveness. This pertains to man's guilt (Romans 3:23) with its resultant condemnation (John 3:18) and death (Romans 5:12; 6:23). The believer is fully forgiven; he is no longer guilty, no longer under the sentence of condemnation and death (John 5:24; Romans 8:1).

The believer has also been *justified* (Colossians 2:14). As man's Representative, Jesus Christ satisfied the demands of God's law. This work has been imputed to the believer. On this basis the believer is looked upon by God as justified, i.e., as though he had perfectly obeyed God and was therefore perfectly righteous (Romans 5:1, 19; 8:1-4; 10:3, 4).

The final possession, which Paul indicates as belonging to every Christian, is that of *freedom from Satan* (Colossians 2:15). Christ came into our nature to free us from the enemy (Hebrews 2:14, 15;

1 John 3:8). The value and power of His work has been imputed to us. The believer has been set free (Ephesians 1:19–2:6; Colossians 1:13). He no longer belongs to Satan—he belongs to God and irrevocably so.

The remarkable factor here is that the believer possesses all of these spiritual benefits *completely*. He is not half forgiven or half justified. This is what Paul meant by *"complete."* The believer "fully possesses" all of these benefits.

In sharp contrast the Bible exhorts the believer to "seek," "mortify," "put off," and to "put on" (Ephesians 4:24; Colossians 3:1, 5, 8). There are many commandments which specify that the Christian is to "grow" (1 Peter 2:2; 2 Peter 3:18), and to "work out your own salvation" (Philippians 2:12).

The Scripture, therefore addresses the Christian in a two-fold manner. On one hand it instructs him in the permanence of his possession of salvation into which he has been fully brought. On the other hand it exhorts him to develop his "walk" and his "witness." In the former area he is reminded that he is "complete" and in the latter he is always "incomplete."

The instruction in all of this is to the effect that the believer has a two-fold relationship with God. There is the relationship of salvation, in which he is complete; and there is the relationship of sanctification, in which the believer will always be incomplete.


## THE NECESSARY DISTINCTION:
### How is Salvation Related to Sanctification?

In order to understand the Bible and to live successfully, we must clearly distinguish between our salvation and our sanctification. To confuse the two will bring uncertainty and ambiguity into all aspects of life and thought.

This distinction is necessary in order to understand the plan of salvation. The Bible is adamant in its denial that salvation is based on good works. It emphasizes in a great variety of ways that one does not achieve salvation by human endeavor of any type (Matthew 7:21-

23; Luke 18:9-14; Galatians 2:16; 3:11; Ephesians 2:8, 9). Salvation is the gift of God (Romans 6:23) and is received by faith (John 3:36; Ephesians 2:8, 9; 1 John 5:9-13).

It is also necessary to make this distinction in order to live the Christian life successfully. Salvation may be likened to the foundation upon which the Christian life is built as a superstructure. To believe that the foundation is defective, that it must continually be shored up, and that it is in constant danger of disappearing altogether would thoroughly discourage even the most committed Christian.

The Bible is emphatically clear on this point. God has promised to give eternal life to all who believe (John 1:12; 3:36). This life, or salvation, with all the benefits described earlier, is the present possession of all believers (John 10:28; 1 John 5:11, 12). The one who has received Jesus Christ as Lord and Savior is exhorted to take God at His Word in this matter of personal salvation and thereby be fully assured of his acceptance by God (1 John 5:9-13). How we may personally feel about our relationship to God is entirely irrelevant. Our feelings are absolutely no standard whatsoever. The only standard is what God has said in His Word. *"These things* have I written unto you that believe . . . that ye may *know* that ye have eternal life . . ."(1 John 5:13).

At this point many earnest Christians confuse the witness of the Holy Spirit and their feelings. They believe, when they lose their "feeling" of assurance, that they have lost the witness of the Holy Spirit. The only conclusion they can draw is that they are not true believers. It is very important for us to recognize that the witness of the Holy Spirit is not our feeling. The "witness" is the Holy Spirit's instruction to us that God has authoritatively spoken in His Word (John 14:26; 15:26; 16:13-15; Romans 8:15, 16; Galatians 4:6; 1 John 5:9-13). The Holy Spirit has *not* been sent to make the believer "feel" that he is a Christian. He was sent to bear witness to Jesus Christ and the Scripture and *on that basis* to lead the believer into the assurance of salvation. Therefore, the Holy Spirit "witnesses" within the believer that the Scripture is true.

To doubt God's Word and work because of personal feeling is a very dishonoring thing to do. God is truth. He is the sovereign Lord. He is worthy of all trust and confidence. He has given us His Word.

36

We must accept His Word, believe what He has said about us and our salvation, and obey His commandments. When we do so we are cooperating with the Holy Spirit.

Having recognized that the salvation foundation of our life is complete and permanent, we may then confidently assume responsibility for the superstructure.


## THE BIBLICAL DESCRIPTION:
### The Characteristics of Salvation and Sanctification.

In salvation the Christian has a "standing" before God which is complete (Colossians 2:10). In contrast, the *daily life* of sanctification is not complete and may be described as his "state."[1] The believer's "standing" is based on the divine work of *imputation*. That is, God simply gives the believing sinner all the salvation benefits purchased for him by Jesus Christ. The believer's "state" is based on the divine work of *impartation*. Here God continually gives to the believer those virtues and enablements which he is spiritually able to receive and practice.

The *first characteristic* which enables one to distinguish between salvation and progressive sanctification is that the former is a *gift* while the latter is *earned*. The benefits of salvation, some of which have been listed earlier, are freely given to all who believe on Jesus Christ as Lord and Savior. They cannot be purchased, or merited, nor are they the product of some natural endowment or heritage. They can only be personally received (Romans 6:23; Ephesians 2:8, 9).

In contrast to the benefits of salvation, those of progressive sanctification must in a sense be *earned*. We receive such virtues and

---

[1]We see a difference between POSITIONAL and PROGRESSIVE sanctification. *Positionally* the believer is completely sanctified. He is "in Christ" (Romans 8:1). His standing is unimpeachable as is his standing in salvation. But his state is often far from satisfactory. As to their standing the Corinthian believers were "saints" (1 Corinthians 1:2) but as to their state they were "carnal" (1 Corinthians 3:3). *Progressively* we should be bringing our state into conformity with our standing and this is done by the power of the cleansing Word (Ephesians 5:26) and the power of the Holy Spirit (Romans 8:13). The author is discussing here progressive sanctification.—Editor.

abilities only as we learn how to put them into practice by faith and love (Romans 6:16; 1 Peter 1:22). An illustration of such a benefit would be the ability to resist temptation. We earn this ability by truly desiring it, by claiming the provision and promise of God (1 Corinthians 10:13), and then by making use of it in acts of faith (Matthew 4:3-11; Hebrews 2:14-18; James 1:2, 12-14; 1 Peter 1:6, 7; 2 Peter 2:9).

The *second characteristic* indicates that the benefit of salvation admit of *no* degrees which the benefits of sanctification, by contrast, *do* admit of degrees. Such a benefit of salvation as forgiveness, is fully given by God. To possess forgiveness at all, in the area of salvation, is to possess it fully (Colossians 2:13; Hebrews 10:19). All believers possess forgiveness in the same degree—completely. This is also true for justification, eternal life, adoption, and all such benefits.

That which the believer possesses by way of progressive sanctification is never complete. Whatever the benefit may be, it is only partially known and utilized. One Christian may possess the ability to resist temptation only in a very small degree while another may possess it in a much larger degree. All Christians have some ability to resist temptation, but all in a different degree.

The *third characteristic* distinction between the provisions of salvation and progressive sanctification is that the former are *permanent* and the latter may be *transitory*. The provisions of salvation are, happily, permanent. We receive these benefits as a gift, they admit of no degrees, and they are ours permanently. This comforting truth is implied in the type of life which God gives to those who believe: it is "eternal" life. Jesus Christ said, "And I give unto them eternal life; and they shall never perish . . ." (John 10:28). We do not merit these benefits of salvation nor do we keep them by merit.

By comparison, the virtues and abilities of progressive sanctification are not necessarily permanent. It is very possible to attain a high degree of progress in some area of Christian practice and then to lose it through neglect. It is debatable whether one may lose any benefit of progressive sanctification absolutely. Undoubtedly this would not be true. Every Christian, however, has experienced remarkable growth in some area only to find a stunting of that growth, and a decline in ability, due to carelessness (1 Corinthians 3:1-4; 5:1-13; 6:1-8; 11:18-

22; 2 Thessalonians 3:6-15; 2 Timothy 4:10).

The *fourth characteristic* which distinguishes between the benefits of salvation and progressive sanctification has to do with their source. The benefits of salvation depend *only* on the Person and work of Jesus Christ. Through His representative work, which has been considered earlier, He obtained all the provisions of salvation. These are given to all who believe, as a gift. They admit of no degrees; they are ours permanently, and they depend only on Jesus Christ (Romans 3:20-31; 5:6-11; 8:1-4, 31-39; Philippians 1:6).

In sharp contrast, the benefits of progressive sanctification depend not only on Jesus Christ and His work, but *also* upon the spiritual cooperation of the believer. It has been pointed out earlier that one must desire and learn how to utilize these benefits. This must also be emphasized here. The provision has been made by Jesus Christ so that His people may live successfully. The Holy Spirit has been sent to teach and anoint the believer. But it is clear from the Scripture and from the experience of every Christian, that our cooperation is necessary.

When we desire to obey God, learn how to submit to His authority and how to put the Bible into daily practice, then the grace and power of God will flow into our lives. "But God be thanked, that ye were the servants of sin, but ye have obeyed from the heart that form of doctrine which was delivered you. Being then made free from sin, ye became the servants of righteousness" (Romans 6:17, 18).

When you have mastered this lesson, take the first part of Exam 3 (covering lesson 4), questions 1-10 on pages 47-49 (right after lesson 5). Remember, you will not turn this exam in for correction until after you have done lesson 5.

# The Biblical Provision for Sanctification

## THE PRACTICAL QUESTION:
### "Is Sanctification an Experience, a Relationship, or a Person?"

The answer to this practical question is that sanctification is all three, but in the reverse order. Primarily, sanctification finds its *source* in the Person of Jesus Christ. *He* has been made our "sanctification" (1 Corinthians 1:30).

No Christian can cleanse himself from sin and no Christian can produce holiness entirely by his own effort. Only God through His grace can do that. Many earnest Christians have met with great frustration and disappointment in attempting, through a lack of understanding, to sanctify themselves.

This in no way may be taken as an excuse to live a careless, carnal, indifferent Christian life. The believer is under the solemn obligation to live free from sin by learning how to go to God in confession for cleansing and to live in holiness of life by learning how to make decisions of faith in appropriating the Person and work of Jesus Christ.

When these two interrelated truths are learned and practiced, then He who is our sanctification will fulfill His will ". . . even your sanctification . . ." (1 Thessalonians 4:3).

Holiness in daily life is not produced, therefore, by resolutions, self-discipline, or any clenching-of-the-teeth attitude alone. Determination and committal are important but are not enough. Holiness is produced by God through His grace.

Sanctification is therefore the result of a *relationship*. When Jesus Christ, our sanctification, is given His rightful place in our life, the effect of His presence and grace will be evident.

Sanctification is not automatic. The daily life of many Christians testifies to that. It is also evident that sanctification is not a once-for-all decision such as salvation. It was shown earlier that the benefits of sanctification must be earned, they are possessed in a variety of degrees, they are transitory benefits, and they also depend on our cooperation with God. To summarize this would indicate that sanctification is progressive. Our growth in grace is a daily matter. The basic issues of the Christian life must be maintained by daily decisions.

What are these daily decisions which we must make? Christianity, we have seen, is demanding. We have been commanded to surrender ourselves, as a person, to God. The issue is not our money, time, pleasures, or even our sins. We are to surrender *ourselves* as a living sacrifice (Mark 8:34; Romans 12:1). Sanctification does not pertain primarily to our money or sins. It has to do with the person who spends the money and commits the sins. It is the *person* who is in need.

We are to surrender ourselves to *God*. Not to the church, nor to Christian service, nor to a certain way of life. We have been commanded to give the control, the authority, the rule of our persons to Another. It is not enough to mouth a few words and to shed a few tears.

This surrender to God is the most important decision in progressive sanctification. Many Christians have done so only superficially. They have made a hasty, shallow, partial surrender and have been deceived as a result. In such cases a Christian may give up some particular sin or habit, he may yield a certain area of his life to God, may accept some activity of his church as important, or he may resolve to live a better life. All of this is important but irrelevant to the basic issue. The Biblical command is inescapable. There is no substitute for the total surrender of the self.

To be a sinner means to be one's own authority. It means to arrogate to ourselves the position of God. This must be recognized, confessed and reversed. We may no longer play God in our own lives or the lives of others. For sanctification to be meaningful in our life it must grow out of a *relationship with Jesus Christ*. This relationship is rooted and grounded only in a complete and honest surrender.

Once this decision has been correctly made it must be maintained on a daily basis. The relationship must now be translated into a daily practice. To surrender ourselves to God not only means that we give Him the control of our inner life, but that all areas of life must be recognized as belonging to Him. Our surrender to Him must be maintained in our motives, ambitions, pleasures, thoughts, evaluations, beliefs, and activities. This is why daily decisions which acknowledge divine Lordship are so important.

And now it is evident that sanctification is also an *experience*. One must accept the authority of God as He has spoken in His Word and learn how to put the Bible into practice in daily life. Sanctification must be a part of our *total experience*.

This does not mean that we become enslaved to rules. The opposite is true. The Christian who has surrendered Himself to God and has learned to practice the principles of sanctification is under servitude only to God. He is free. This, on the other hand, does not make him irresponsible to the Bible, the church, Christian service, and the needs and feelings of others. In all these ways he will learn to express his love to God. Love for God and obedience to the Word of God, as we have seen, are inseparable (John 14:15; 1 John 5:3).


## THE DOCTRINAL QUESTION:
### "How is Sanctification Related to the Work of Christ?"

Every benefit of the gospel, including sanctification, has been provided for the Christian by Jesus Christ through His crucifixion, resurrection, ascension, and the sending of the Holy Spirit on the day of Pentecost.

It is important to understand that, in each of these historical deeds, Christ provided for *more* than the believer's initial salvation.

In *the crucifixion* the believer has been justified, delivered from condemnation, and reconciled to God (Romans 5:6-11). All of this pertains to the gift of salvation. Jesus Christ died as the believer's substitute. He took upon Himself the condemnation and judgment which had been justly passed upon mankind. He died under the wrath of God so that the believer may never experience that wrath. Redemption has been obtained. There is a complete, legal forgiveness of sins (Ephesians 1:7; Colossians 2:13; Hebrews 10:17).

However, Jesus Christ not only died that man may be redeemed. He died that the believer may be able to live a successful Christian life. And this is what the Scriptures call "sanctification."

In His crucifixion, Jesus Christ has provided a *cleansing* from the power, influence, and effect of the believer's sinful nature. This nature is called in Scripture the "old man" (Romans 6:6; Ephesians 4:22; Colossians 3:9). In His death, as the believer's representative, Jesus Christ brought the fallen nature of man under the judgment of God (Romans 6:6). A cleansing has therefore been obtained, so that the believer may be free from the sinful nature which he yet possesses and which is the source of so much of his spiritual defeat (Romans 6:6-22).

In the Scripture some aspects of both salvation and sanctification are also related to *the resurrection* of Jesus Christ.

In regard to salvation, the believer's justification (Romans 4:25), spiritual birth (1 Peter 1:3), and future resurrection (1 Corinthians 15: 20-58) are shown to have their source in Christ's resurrection.

The sanctification benefits of the resurrection are also clearly stated in the Scriptures. The Apostle Paul spoke of his desire to experience the power of the resurrection in daily life (Philippians 3:10). And he prayed for the Christians at Ephesus that they would know this same power (Ephesians 1:19, 20). What Paul is referring to is the *enablement* which Christ provided through His resurrection so that the believer may live with spiritual virtue, grace, and power in his life. This is described in the Bible as being ". . . alive unto God . . ." (Romans 6:11).

The believer, therefore, need not live with doubt in his life. He may have, through Christ's resurrection, the virtue of faith. Instead of pessimism and discouragement, he may have hope. And instead of bitterness, estrangement, and selfishness, he may have love (1 Corinthians 13; 1 Thessalonians 1:3). Again the list of practical benefits is endless (Galatians 5:22, 23; Ephesians 4:22-32; Philippians 4:5-8; Colossians 3:10-17).

To *the ascension* of Jesus Christ the Bible also attributes some benefits of both salvation and sanctification.

In the area of salvation Jesus Christ ascended into heaven to be the believer's forerunner (Hebrews 6:19, 20) and intercessor (Hebrews 7:25; 8:1; 9:24). The Apostle Paul also indicated that the believer has been given the position of authority over Satan by means of Christ's ascension (Ephesians 1:19-23). He is "seated in the heavenlies" in Jesus Christ (Ephesians 2:5, 6).

This position of authority provides daily *deliverance* from Satan. This deliverance must now be put into practice in the believer's sanctification. He is commanded to guard against allowing Satan some sinful opportunity in his life (Ephesians 4:27) and to deliberately appropriate all the benefits of his relationship with Christ so he may be able to resist the Devil (Ephesians 6:10-18; 1 Peter 5:8, 9). The Christian has not only been crucified in and with Christ (Galatians 2:20); he has been raised from the grave and has ascended in the Person of His Representative (Ephesians 2:5, 6; Colossians 3:1-3). The spiritual benefits of his position, when practiced by the Christian, are a part of his progressive sanctification.

On the *day of Pentecost* the ascended Lord Jesus Christ bestowed the Holy Spirit upon all those who were believers (Acts 2:33). In a similar way to the other three deeds of atonement, the believer has a two-fold relationship to the Person and work of the Holy Spirit.

It is the Holy Spirit who convicts the non-Christian of his sinful and lost condition (John 16:7-11). He brings the convicted person into the benefits of the new birth through the gift of repentance and faith (John 3:3-5; 2 Thessalonians 2:13; 1 Peter 1:2). The Holy Spirit protects and preserves the new believer as His indwelling "seal" (2 Corinthians 1:22; Ephesians 1:13, 14; 4:30) and makes him a member of the "body of Christ" (Romans 12:4, 5; 1 Corinthians 12:13). The believer becomes the "temple" of the Holy Spirit (1 Corinthians 3:16, 17; 6:19).

As related to sanctification the Holy Spirit resides in the believer to be his "Comforter" (Helper) in a continual *anointing* (John 14:16, 17, 26; 16:13, 14; 1 John 2:27). While Jesus Christ is the believer's *Sanctification,* it is the Holy Spirit who is his *Sanctifier.* It is He who leads the believer in his progressive freedom from the sinfulness of his fallen nature (Romans 8:13; Galatians 5:16-18) through an understanding of the Scripture and its daily practice in obedience to God (1 Peter 1:22). The Holy Spirit witnesses to the believer concerning the authenticity of the Word of God and assures him on that basis of his relationship to God (1 John 5:6-13; Romans 8:15, 16; Galatians 4:6). He undergirds the Christian in his prayer life (Romans 8:26, 27) and gives him spiritual gifts so that he might adequately serve God (Romans 12:3-8; 1 Corinthians 12:1-11; Ephesians 4:7-16).

The Christian is commanded not to grieve or quench the Holy Spirit by resisting His leading (Ephesians 4:30; 1 Thessalonians 5:19) but to be constantly filled with the Spirit through daily obedience (Ephesians 5:18).

In summary, then, Jesus Christ, through His atonement, has made an adequate spiritual provision for every area of the believer's daily life. He has provided a daily *cleansing* through His crucifixion, a daily *enablement* through His resurrection, a daily *deliverance* through His ascension, and a daily *anointing* through Pentecost. It is very important for the Christian to understand this.

The Christian who lives and prays in ambiguity is doomed to failure and disappointment in daily life.

When you are ready, complete Exam 3 by answering questions 11-20 on pages 49-51. (You should have already answered questions 1-10 as part of your study of lesson 4.)

When you have answered all the questions in Exam 3, mail the exam for correction.

HIGHER GROUND

Exam
Name _____ Grade_____
(print plainly)

Address _____

Zip                    Class
City_____ State _____ Code _____ Number _____

Instructor _____

## LESSON 4

*In the blank space in the right-hand margin write the letter of the correct answer.*

1. A person is assured of a perfect standing before God as and
   when he
   a. lives a good, moral and upright life
   b. becomes an active member of the church
   c. personally believes on the Lord Jesus as Savior from sin
   d. does all the above                                _____

2. When the New Testament speaks of the believer as being
   "complete" in Christ, it uses a word which signifies
   a. *ultimate* completeness
   b. "to possess fully"
   c. "to make up that which is lacking"
   d. "paid in full"                                    _____

3. When Paul speaks of a person being "quickened" he means
   that this person
   a. has made rapid progress in his Christian life
   b. has a tender conscience toward things which grieve the
      Holy Spirit.
   c. easily grasps spiritual truth
   d. has been made alive spiritually                   _____

**4.** When the New Testament speaks of a believer being "forgiven" or "justified" or "delivered from Satan," it
a. always qualifies the statement with a condition
b. always distinguishes between those blessings which are conditional and those which are unconditional
c. usually implies the eternal state of the believer rather than any present condition
d. speaks of these things as being the full and complete possession of the believer here and now _____

**5.** Which of the following is true of the Christian?
a. He is, paradoxically, both complete and incomplete
b. He is perfect as to his eternal standing yet imperfect as to his present state
c. His salvation is fixed and final; his sanctification is progressive and incomplete
d. All the above are true _____

**6.** Assurance of salvation depends on
a. how hard we work to maintain it
b. how we feel at any given moment
c. the finished work of Christ as confirmed in the written word of God
d. whether or not we keep the ordinances Christ left with His Church _____

**7.** The function of the Holy Spirit is to
a. give us the feelings of joy, peace and well-being which accompany any true conversion experience
b. impart to us an ecstatic experience on which we can base our assurance with confidence
c. witness to Christ and on that ground alone impart to the believer assurance of salvation
d. assure the believer of his salvation independently and entirely apart from the Bible _____

**8.** The believer's standing before God depends on
a. the benefits of the work of Christ imputed to him by God
b. what is imparted to him by the indwelling Holy Spirit
c. both the above
d. neither of the above _____

**9.** Which of the following makes room for degrees or stages of development?
a. Salvation
b. Sanctification
c. Justification
d. Adoption _____

**10.** Which of the following can a truly born-again believer lose, to a greater or lesser degree, through neglect?
   a. His salvation
   b. The indwelling of the Holy Spirit
   c. His degree of development in a given area of his Christian life
   d. All of the above                                           _____

## WHAT DO YOU SAY?

How do you know you are truly saved?

_____

_____

_____

_____

_____

## LESSON 5

*In the blank space in the right-hand margin write the letter of the correct answer.*

**11.** In this lesson, sanctification is set forth as an experience, a relationship, and a Person. In logical order, the first of these is
   a. the experience
   b. the relationship
   c. the Person
   d. none of them; they are all of prime importance and do not lend themselves to arrangement in order                    _____

**12.** Since Christ is "made unto us sanctification," that
   a. absolves us of any responsibility to live a life free from sin
   b. makes it imperative that we should try hard to live up to His standards of holiness
   c. guarantees that practical sanctification is a permanent condition and one which is imputed to us fully and without cooperation on our part
   d. should result in a clean life made possible by appropriating for ourselves the Person and work of Christ            _____

**13.** Holiness of life is produced by
  a. determination and self discipline
  b. committal to Christ alone
  c. God through His grace as we cooperate by giving Christ His rightful place in our lives
  d. an automatic process, the natural outworking of salvation by faith through grace _____

**14.** The key to practical sanctification is the daily surrender to God of
  a. ourselves as persons
  b. our money and possessions
  c. our sins and shortcomings
  d. our time and opportunities _____

**15.** It would be true to say that
  a. a partial surrender to God is better than no surrender at all
  b. a partial surrender to God is actually deceptive
  c. a true surrender to God may be equated with the resolve to live a better life
  d. a total surrender to God is impossible to achieve _____

**16.** A true surrender to God is
  a. a once-for-all experience
  b. something which must be kept up daily
  c. something which involves the inner life only
  d. bound to result in a life bounded by rigid rules
  e. an emancipating experience which frees the believer from any obligation to attend church
  f. something to be feared since it might result in God asking us to do something or go somewhere which would clash with our own desires _____

**17.** The "old man" is
  a. a Biblical term describing the sinful nature with which we are born
  b. completely eradicated, in a true Christian, at conversion
  c. an ever-present reality in the life of the most devout believer and one from which there can be escape in this life
  d. a problem to most Christians but can be overcome by culti-vating one's good points and repressing the bad ones _____

**18.** The intercessory work of the Lord Jesus on the believer's behalf is connected, in Scripture, with His
   a. crucifixion
   b. resurrection
   c. ascension
   d. second coming                                             _____

**19.** Positionally, the believer in Christ is seated with Christ in the heavenlies. This means that the believer
   a. is already in the only heaven spoken of in Scripture
   b. has power over the Devil
   c. cannot possibly commit sin
   d. has only blessings to enjoy and no battles to fight so long as he appropriates this truth                         _____

**20.** The believer should regard his body as
   a. evil and a continual hindrance to holy living
   b. the temple of the Holy Spirit
   c. "the body of Christ"
   d. something he will leave behind at death never to possess again                                                      _____

## WHAT DO YOU SAY?

Describe one work of the Holy Spirit which has been particularly helpful to you in living the Christian life.

_____

_____

_____

_____

_____

*MAIL TO address shown on back outside cover.*
*PLEASE enclose a stamped addressed envelope for the return of your corrected exam.*

# The Crucifixion in the Believer's Daily Life

## THE CRUCIFIXION:
## The "Old Man" and the Need of Cleansing.

The believer has been delivered once for all from the guilt of his sin—that is salvation. Now he needs to be progressively delivered from the power of sin—that is sanctification.

To be successful Christians we must recognize our problems, understand them and learn to overcome them. The first and most formidable problem which stands in the Christian's path of success is *himself*.

The Christian is a sinful person. He not only commits sins—he has a sinful nature. The committing of sins is only the superficial evidence of the underlying nature. And this is where the problem lies—not with the deeds but with their cause and source. The Christian needs a deliverance, a cleansing, from the nature which is inseparable from himself.

But this presents an almost insurmountable problem—to acknowledge that we are at fault. It is exceedingly difficult for the believer to confess that he is in need of help. It is far easier to blame our failures on a lack of time, money, education, background, intelligence or personality. It is far easier to place the blame on parents, fellow-workers, roommates, wife or husband, pastor, or even God!

Our sinful pride is often much more important and valuable to us than the glory of God and our personal success as Christians.

"Now don't blame that on me, I'm a person of spiritual integrity," is more often heard and implied than, "I was at fault," "I'm sorry I said that," "I need your forgiveness," or, "I am a sinful person and need help."

To be cleansed from my pride, lust, envy, jealousy, covetousness, dishonesty, and bigotry I must acknowledge and confess that I am a proud person, a lustful person, an envious person, a jealous person, a covetous person, a dishonest person, a bigot. This confession must be genuine. It must be more than words. It must be a truthful appraisal in the presence of God.

The way in which we begin with ourselves is to admit and confess that we need the cleansing God has promised (Romans 6:14; 1 John 1:9). We must open up our persons to God and allow Him to deal with us. This is absolutely necessary.

First of all, the Christian needs a divine cleansing from the power of the sinful nature—because of *what it is*. He has a nature which is at enmity with God (Romans 8:7)! The seriousness of this and its far-reaching effects cannot be overemphasized. The Christian must face the inescapable truth that he belongs to God and must obey God, and yet possesses a nature which is thoroughly antagonistic to all that is holy and loving and true. He has a built-in hindrance to any genuine progress in the Christian life. His nature will approve of lust but not purity, of pride but not humility—the list is endless.

It is not easy for the Christian to admit the sinfulness of his own nature. The Bible, however, is clear on this point (Jeremiah 17:9; Romans 1:19-32; 3:10-18) and so is our daily experience, if we are willing to look. We must admit that our first reaction to a new truth from the Scripture is one of resistance. It is much easier to find ten reasons why we should not obey God than simply to obey! Give the ordinary Christian five seconds and he can rationalize almost any of his vices into virtues!

Because of this nature and its warfare against God, the non-Christian is described as an enemy of God (Romans 5:10). Even in the Christian this sinful nature continues its opposition to God and therefore to the believer's spiritual progress. No wonder the Christian catches himself disliking God! How quickly and easily he can sit in judgment on God and refuse to accept some teaching of the Bible because of personal disapproval!

Such a description of our nature is in no way intended to imply that man is as bad as he *can* be nor that man cannot do civil good or approve of the good. This, however, is not to be traced to man's nature but to the common and special grace of God.

Our sinful nature, the "old man," cannot be brought under subjugation to the will of God (Romans 8:7). No amount of prayer, Bible study, decisions of faith, self-discipline, church attendance, and Christian service will change the old nature. What the Christian must do is to learn not to obey his sinful nature. The Scripture is very clear on this point. The command is not to *change* the old nature but to *reject* it (Ephesians 4:22; Colossians 3:5-9).

The second reason why the Christian needs to be cleansed from the power of his old nature is because of *what it does*. The Lord Jesus taught His disciples that one was "defiled" by what *came out* of man and not by that which *went in* (Mark 7:17-23). When we accept the prompting of our sinful nature, and put the suggestion into practice, the result is an action or activity out of harmony with the will of God. This expressing of the "old man" is what "defiles" us. The tragic products of the old nature are not only clearly seen in the Bible (Mark 7:21, 22; Romans 1:21-32; Galatians 5:19-21) but, in some measure, in the lives of all Christians. Our pride, hypocrisy, jealousy, deceit, selfishness, and lust are easily discernible. So are our lack of love, lack of faith, and lack of hope.

Augustine emphasized the Biblical principle that the judgment for sin is inexorably connected with the sin itself (*Confessions,* Book I, par. 19). When sin is committed, the sinner, whether Christian or non-Christian, becomes directly influenced by the sin. Our character is changed by our deliberate choice to disobey God and to practice evil. We become characterized by the nature of our sin! Therefore, in the Bible, the one who steals is described as a "thief," the one who is immoral is an "adulterer," and the one who gossips is a "tale-bearer." When we choose to obey our sinful nature, the resultant activity will "enslave" us (John 8:34; Romans 7:15-18, 23, 24).

A third reason why the Christian should learn how to appropriate the divine provision for his old nature, is because of *what it does not do*. It is never a help in the Christian life. Not one victory, not one genuine desire for God, not one holy or loving thought or activity can be traced back to the old nature (Romans 7:18, 23). This alone should be reason enough for the Christian to seek how he may live in freedom from his fallen nature.

A final reason why the earnest believer must give heed to what the Scripture states about his old nature, is because of *the commandment* of God. The Christian has been commanded to "put off . . . the old man" (Ephesians 4:22).

This leaves us with no correct alternative but that of obedience. The Christian, therefore, may not live in unconcern about the manifestation of the old nature in his life. God must be obeyed.


## THE CRUCIFIXION:
### The "Old Man" and the Provision for Cleansing.

If it is true that the Christian possesses a nature which is at enmity with God, which cannot be brought into subjection to the will of God, which defiles and enslaves, which is never the source of spiritual help, and a nature which he has been commanded by God to reject—then the Christian must seek to understand the provision God has made and to practice it.

In the crucifixion such a provision for cleansing from the power of the old nature has been made (Romans 6:1-10). The Apostle Paul affirms that the sinful nature, possessed by every believer, has been judged in the death of Jesus Christ. Acting as our representative, Christ took our nature to His cross so that we may be free from its influence. In His death the "old man" was legally stripped of its power.

It is important for us to understand that we were identified with Jesus Christ in His death. "I am crucified with Christ. . ." may not only be said by the Apostle Paul but by every believer (Galatians 2:20). We were there when our Lord was crucified and we were crucified in and with Him (Romans 6:1-10; Colossians 2:10-15; 3:1-3).

The value of this deliverance has been imputed to the believer.

When you have mastered this lesson, take the first part of Exam 4 (covering lesson 6), questions 1-10 on pages 67-68 (right after lesson 7). Remember, you will not turn this exam in for correction until after you have done lesson 7.

He is, therefore, described in the Bible as being "dead to sin" (Romans 6:2, 7; Colossians 3:3). The Apostle Paul explains this statement in Romans six. It means to possess freedom from sin (Romans 6:1-11). His reference here is not to forgiveness but to freedom from the *power* of the "old man."

Every believer possesses this freedom legally. We may not understand this nor manifest this freedom in any large measure in our lives. It is ours, however, simply because we are believers. The old nature of every believer, our greatest personal hindrance to the success of our Christian life, has been judged by God; it has been stripped of its power, and we have been set free. The old nature was crucified with Jesus Christ.

## THE CRUCIFIXION:
### The "Old Man" and the Conditions for Cleansing.

What the believer possesses legally he must learn to practice in daily life. It is not enough to have an account in the bank. We must learn to write the check.

God has made a provision for our cleansing. The power of this provision, however, will not flow into our daily life until we understand the conditions for cleansing and choose to practice them.

The Apostle Paul stated that there were three conditions we must meet. The first revolves around the word "reckon" (Romans 6:11). This indicates that we must make a decision to act in harmony with and on the basis of the atoning work of Christ. We legally died in and with Jesus Christ. Now we must choose to *put into practice* the provision and principle of the crucifixion—no matter what it may cost.

The second condition is a decision to *live* free from the old nature (Romans 6:12). There is no deliverance when we choose to live in sin or call it by some other name. No amount of tears, prayer, agony, and spiritual work can substitute for the simple decision to obey God and to forsake the sin.

The third condition is a decision to *trust* God by yielding to Him (Romans 6:13). This is a *deliberate dependence* on God for the grace necessary to practice the first two decisions. Here the necessity of Biblical faith needs to be emphasized. Sanctification is not brainwashing or wish-fulfillment. It is the work of God in the believer. Without faith it is impossible to please God (Hebrews 11:6). These three decisions which form the conditions for our cleansing are all decisions of faith.

The important question now is how to apply these three decisions to our daily life. What do they mean in practice?

First of all we must acknowledge our own personal need of divine help. Personal involvement is absolutely necessary. No sinner is ever forgiven until he confesses that he is a sinner and no saint is ever cleansed without his acknowledgment of personal need. We must accept what God has said about our old nature (Romans 7:14-24; 8:7) and assume responsibility to obey the commandment to reject the old nature (Ephesians 4:22).

The second step in deliverance is the necessity of being specific in confession. The old nature manifests itself in *specific* sins (Galatians 5:19-21; Colossians 3:5-9). These must be recognized and confessed as such to God. To call our sins by any other name and to relate ourselves to them by rationalization instead of by confession will make freedom and cleansing an impossibility! When we have been proud, the only recourse is to point our spiritual finger at that sin and call it "pride." When we have gossipped, we must name it for what it is and confess before God that we are a "gossipper." For most Christians this is indeed difficult. Our pride and arrogancy are often much more important than the will and power and glory of God. Without confession, however, there is no cleansing (1 John 1:9).

The third step is that of forsaking our sin. Having confessed an activity as sinful, we are left with no alternative but that of thoroughly renouncing the sin. What may an earnest Christian do with his sin but to forsake it? The only thing that would ever be worse than committing a sin would be to continue to practice it—once its true nature is known. To confess a sin and then not to forsake it is evidence that our confession was false!

The fourth step is to receive Jesus Christ as the specific cleansing we may need. *He* is our sanctification (1 Corinthians 1:30). When we

were in need of salvation, we received a Person—Jesus Christ Savior. In sanctification the principle is the same (Colossian He is not only our sanctification in general but also in all those areas where sin is committed and where sanctification must the be practiced. The cleansing which Jesus Christ has provided is arable from His Person. This is not only true in salvation but in sa cation. God has promised to cleanse us when we truly confess o (1 John 1:9). Jesus Christ is our cleansing (Romans 7:24, 25; P pians 1:11). It is necessary to be exceeding specific at this p "Lord Jesus, I confess that I sinned against You in that act of p I am a proud person. I choose to forsake my pride by Your grace claiming Your promise I receive You as my cleansing from the si pride."

The fifth step is to believe God and to live as a cleansed pers This step, as all the others, is a decision of faith. God has promised cleanse us from unrighteousness (1 John 1:9). Having claimed t promise we must act accordingly. God expects us to take Him at H Word. Any doubt as to whether we have been cleansed is out o harmony with the faithfulness of God and the truthfulness of His Word When temptation comes we must reaffirm our previous decision. The temptation must be rejected in that the sin has already been confessed, forsaken, and cleansing has been received.

When these steps of sanctification are put into practice, the grace and power of God will flow into our lives. When we obey—God works. This principle of sanctification is found throughout the Bible (Philippians 2:12, 13; 1 Peter 1:22). Obedience produces freedom from sin and righteousness in daily life (Romans 6:16-18).

Only God can deal with sin and only God can produce holiness. The Christian must learn how to make these decisions of faith so the power and grace of the crucifixion may be present in his life. And, having made these decisions of faith, he must learn to say, "No," to his old nature.

The crucifixion is a historical event. Jesus Christ died to free the believer from the power of his old nature. The believer died in Christ. The crucifixion indicated God's disapproval of the old nature. The believer may not live as though this did not happen.

# The Resurrection in the Believer's Daily Life

## THE RESURRECTION:
### The "New Man" and the Need of Enablement.

The provision of cleansing in the crucifixion is largely negative. It is a cleansing *from* the power of the fallen nature. The believer, however, needs more than cleansing. He also needs a divine *enablement* to obey God and to possess and to practice the virtues commended in the Scripture.

Even the most careless reading of the Bible will indicate the importance of obeying God. Throughout the New Testament, obedience is presented as an evidence of salvation. Those who do not practice the commandments and Word of God are not true believers (1 John 2:3-5). Obedience to God is equated with salvation (Hebrews 5:9) and forgiveness (1 Peter 1:2). In the return of Jesus Christ, those who will be judged are described as those who "know not God, and that obey not the gospel of our Lord Jesus Christ" (2 Thessalonians 1:8).

Even more emphatically, obedience is described as a characteristic of sanctification. To love God is to obey Him (John 14:15, 21, 23; 1 John 5:3; 2 John 6). According to Paul and Peter the secret of progressive sanctification is found in the practice of obedience (Romans 6:16-18; Philippians 2:12, 13; 1 Peter 1:14-22). The four great exhortations of sanctification, to "put off" (Ephesians 4:22; Colossians 3:9); "put on" (Ephesians 4:24; Colossians 3:10); "resist" (Ephesians 4:27;

6:11-13; 1 Peter 5:9); and "be filled" (Ephesians 5:18), are amplified and applied throughout the New Testament in principle and precept. There is no substitute nor alternative for obedience.

In regard to sanctification and obedience two things of importance must be kept in mind. The first has to do with motivation. Happy is the person who lives in a culture which demands a morality paralleling the Bible. Not stealing from the neighbor but being kind to him is approved by the Scripture. However if we refrain from stealing simply because of our culture we are not reflecting our sanctification. Even the non-Christian lives according to the demands of culture. Sanctification grows out of a relationship with God—not culture.

It is necessary, therefore, to question our motivation. To act in harmony with the Bible because of our culture, or because of our fear of criticism, or because of our reputation, or because of our desire for success, is surely not an expression of loving obedience to God.

The second factor of importance in regard to sanctification concerns one of its characteristics: *sanctification is positive*. Too often the emphasis is placed upon a negative separation. Many of the commandments of the New Testament do exhort the believer not to engage in certain activities (Ephesians 4:25-31; Colossians 3:5, 8, 9; 1 John 2:15-17). This, however, is so we may be free to give God His rightful place in our lives and to practice His will. In the Scripture sanctification is inseparably related to the positive manifestation in daily life of the virtues of love, faith, and hope (Matthew 22:36-40; 1 Corinthians 13; Hebrews 11:6; 1 Thessalonians 1:3; 3:6; 1 John 3:14-18). It is not enough to *abstain* from loving the world (1 John 2:15); we must *love* God (Matthew 22:37, 38). We must do more than *refrain* from putting faith in ourselves (Jeremiah 17:5; Luke 18:9); we must put our *faith* in God (Jeremiah 17:7; Hebrews 11:6; 1 John 3:23). *Freedom* from despair and pessimism is not sufficient (Romans 4:18); one must practice *hope* in God (Romans 15:13; 1 Peter 1:13).

Sanctification is, therefore, a process whereby the believer is increasingly brought into a spiritual conformity with Jesus Christ (Romans 8:28, 29). For this the Christian needs divine enablement.

# THE RESURRECTION:
## The "New Man" and the Provision of Enablement.

In the New Testament almost all of the positive benefits of salvation and sanctification are traced back to the resurrection of Jesus Christ. In this great deed of God in history, the Lord Jesus Christ not only verified the truthfulness of His divine Sonship (Romans 1:4); presented evidence that His work of atonement was finished and accepted (Acts 13:29-39); assured all men of a future judgment (Acts 17:31) and resurrection (John 5:29; 1 Corinthians 15:20-28; Revelation 20:11-15); but also made adequate provision for the Christian to live in "newness of life" (Romans 6:4).

In his salvation the believer was given spiritual life (John 3:3, 5; 10:10, 28; 17:2; Ephesians 2:5; 1 John 5:11, 12). Through this work of regeneration his character was transformed and he was given a "new nature" (1 Corinthians 6:11; 2 Corinthians 5:17; Galatians 6:15). The believer now has the ability, through his new nature, to say "no" to the old nature with all its evil, and to live with faith, love, hope, and spiritual power, as part of his daily experience. These benefits all find their source in the work of Jesus Christ in His resurrection (Romans 6:4; 7:4; Colossians 2:12, 13; 1 Peter 1:3, 21).

As the recipient of this work of Christ, the believer is described as being "alive unto God" (Romans 6:11) and "married to another" (Romans 7:4). These terms indicate the revolutionary change which has been brought into the life of one who was once dead and alienated from God. They also describe the potential enablement which has been given to every believer.

The Apostle Paul explains this provision as a divine power. He prayed for the Ephesian Christians that they might know this power in their daily lives (Ephesians 1:19, 20) and stated that he sought to live so he might experience the same enablement (Philippians 3:10).

The practical result of this divine provision is that the Christian need no longer live under the dominion of sin nor the influence of the old nature. He has been set free and has the ability to live a life of obedience, righteousness, and holiness (Romans 6:11, 12; Philippians 1:11). Such a life has been described by the Apostle Paul as "bringing forth fruit unto God" (Romans 7:4).

One of the greatest sins and one that is found in the lives of all Christians is our *failure to appropriate the provision God has made available through the resurrection.* It is not the will of God that we live the Christian life in our own strength. He said, "without Me ye can do nothing" (John 15:5).

The Christian stands without excuse before this reality of divine provision.


## THE RESURRECTION:
### The "New Man" and the Conditions for Enablement.

It is one thing to know that Jesus Christ has made an adequate provision for our daily lives but it is quite another to incorporate this provision into our daily practice. What must we do to appropriate this power to live a holy life?

In the crucifixion Jesus Christ provided a cleansing from the believer's old nature. We are therefore exhorted to "put off the old man" (Ephesians 4:22; Colossians 3:9). In the resurrection Jesus Christ provided an enablement to live a holy life through the provision of a new nature. We are therefore exhorted to "put on the new man" (Ephesians 4:24; Colossians 3:10). Until we learn to obey God in this way—we are doomed to spiritual failure. No amount of pious talk or ambiguous praying can be a substitute for clear-cut decisions of faith.

By the use of the term "new man" the Apostle Paul is referring to the new nature and ability which has been given to every believer in his salvation (2 Peter 1:3, 4; Colossians 1:29; Philippians 4:13). This ability to live the Christian life successfully is not automatic; it must be *appropriated by faith.* One must *learn how* to "put on the new man" by deliberate choice and practice.

In the previous chapter we found that the Bible presents three conditions for cleansing from the old nature. These conditions are to be put into practice through five steps which are all decisions of faith. Now, in regard to the resurrection and the new nature, the conditions and the steps are the same but with a *positive* emphasis. The key is found in the Biblical exhortation that, having "put off," we are now to "put on" (Colossians 3:9, 10). The former exhortation refers primarily to the cleansing provided in the crucifixion and the latter to the enablement which is ours in the resurrection.

By a decision of faith we are to "put off," for example, the sin of selfishness and to "put on" the contrasting virtue of love. Or it may be lust, or doubt, or fear, or jealousy that must be rejected by faith and the virtues of purity, faith, courage, or praise to be chosen in their place. The specific sin from which a believer may need cleansing and the specific virtue with which he may need enablement depends upon his spiritual life and circumstances. The hypocrite, for example, needs a different type of enablement than the alcoholic.

We may not live as though the resurrection did not happen. It did happen and God has made adequate provision for our spiritual life. Therefore, we must make the spiritual decision to think and live in harmony with the resurrection (Romans 6:11). We must also make the decision to live in the strength of the new nature (Romans 6:12) and to do so in active dependence on God (Romans 6:13).

These three conditions of success must be put into practice through the five steps mentioned earlier. We must sincerely and honestly *acknowledge our need* of help, *confess our failure* to manifest His grace, deliberately *forsake our sins* of omission, *receive Jesus Christ* as our specific enablement, and then live our daily lives *practicing* the virtues provided in Jesus Christ through the resurrection. These are all necessary decisions of faith.

Without this type of involvement with God and the resurrection, we may expect only failure.

The use of these five steps in regard to the crucifixion and the resurrection is one of emphasis only. In fact, the "putting off" and the "putting on" can be done at the same time. Once the believer learns how to make the decisions of faith, the rejection of selfishness and the appropriation of love may be but the two aspects of the same decision.

The important factor is that the decisions be made and made as a response of genuine surrender and faith in God. Simply stating the words is worse than worthless. Mere platitudes invoke the judgment of God.

When you are ready, complete Exam 4 by answering questions 11-20 on pages 69-71. (You should have already answered questions 1-10 as part of your study of lesson 6.)

When you have answered all the questions in Exam 4, mail the exam for correction.

# HIGHER GROUND

Name_____ Exam
        (print plainly)                         Grade_____

Address _____

                                    Zip          Class
City_____ State _____ Code _____ Number _____

Instructor _____

## LESSON 6

*In the blank space in the right-hand margin write the letter of the correct answer.*

**1.**  When we are at fault the thing to do is to
a. conceal the fact as long as possible
b. admit it and confess to God that we need cleansing
c. deny it since all confession is an admission of weakness
d. give up all further attempts to live a holy life          _____

**2.**  Where does it say in the Bible that God is faithful and just to
forgive and cleanse sins when they are confessed to Him? In
a. John 3:16
b. Acts 4:12
c. Romans 8:9
d. 1 John 1:9          _____

**3.**  Jeremiah 17:9 declares that the human heart
a. is warm, loving and generous
b. is deceitful and bad beyond all knowing
c. is holy, just and good
d. instinctively loves God          _____

**4.**  The sinful nature of the old man
a. can be brought into subjection to the will of God
b. is capable of being reformed if we are willing to make the effort
c. is implacably hostile to God
d. makes it impossible for Christians to do anything pleasing to God
e. ceases to operate once a person becomes a Christian          _____

5. Christians need cleansing from the power of the old nature because of
   a. what it is
   b. what it does
   c. what it does not do
   d. all the above

   _____

6. So far as the old nature is concerned, the Christian
   a. has an option as to whether or not he will renounce it
   b. has been commanded by God to renounce it
   c. has an obligation to put up with it since his failures help keep him humble
   d. has no part to play in ridding himself of it since "Calvary covers it all"

   _____

7. The believer is judicially "dead to sin." In its Biblical context this means that
   a. the old nature has been stripped of its power
   b. when a believer sins he ceases to be a Christian because thereafter he is "dead in sin"
   c. he is no longer able to sin
   d. when he dies a believer will be taken to heaven

   _____

8. The conditions for cleansing and holy living include
   a. deliberate counting on what God has said and on what Christ has done
   b. deciding to live free from the old nature
   c. depending on God for the ability to practice a holy life
   d. all the above

   _____

9. When confessing failure to the Lord Jesus it is necessary to be
   a. vague rather than specific at all times
   b. exceedingly specific at all times
   c. specific when it comes to sins of the flesh but general when it comes to sins of the spirit
   d. specific if it is a sin against another Christian but general if it is a sin against God

   _____

10. Which of the following best summarizes the basic principle of progressive sanctification?
    a. Praying through works wonders
    b. The harder we try the easier it becomes
    c. If at first you don't succeed, try again
    d. When we obey, God works
    e. Never say die

    _____

## WHAT DO YOU SAY?

What has been your experience since putting into practice the principles taught in this lesson?

_____

_____

_____

_____

_____

## LESSON 7

*In the blank space in the right-hand margin write the letter of the correct answer.*

**11.** The Bible teaches that those who do *NOT* keep Christ's commandments
   a. are not true Christians
   b. are a minority of professing Christians
   c. are to be excused on the grounds that Christ's commandments are impractical in this age
   d. are backsliders                                    _____

**12.** Which is a basic characteristic of practical and progressive sanctification?
   a. Sinless perfection
   b. Continuing obedience
   c. Unbroken victory
   d. Deep introspection                                 _____

**13.** To refrain from doing things frowned upon by the culture which surrounds us is
   a. not necessarily an evidence of sanctification
   b. quite evidently one proof that we are living sanctified lives
   c. merely to emphasize the negative side of sanctification
   d. a mandatory requirement of true sanctification     _____

**14.** What place does separation have in our sanctification? It
a. has no place at all since it is entirely negative and such prohibitions as "taste not, touch not, handle not" have no part in vital Christianity
b. is a great imperative which should govern all Christian relationships but it really has no direct link with sanctification
c. is the negative side of sanctification and is commanded so that we might be liberated from things displeasing to God thus making the positive side of sanctification possible
d. relates more to salvation than to sanctification for until a person is willing to give up his sins he cannot be saved at all _____

**15.** When a Christian has learned to abstain from places, practices and pleasures which hinder his growth in the Christian life, he has
a. discharged all his obligations Godward
b. arrived at a plateau of sanctification reached by only a relative few
c. yet to "put on" certain virtues and be made like the Lord Jesus in a positive way
d. to maintain ceaseless watchfulness lest he slip back into his old way of life and be guilty of apostasy _____

**16.** The believer is said to be "alive unto God" and this makes it potentially possible for him to be sanctified in life. This truth is invariably linked with
a. the immaculate conception of the Lord Jesus Christ
b. the spotless, sinless humanity of the Lord Jesus
c. the vicarious, efficacious and substitutionary death of Christ
d. the glorious, triumphant resurrection of Christ _____

**17.** The failure of Christians to appropriate God's provision for holy living is described in this lesson as
a. a tragedy
b. one of the great sins a Christian can commit
c. an indictment of the church for its failure to teach the whole truth of the gospel
d. sad commentary on the smugness of twentieth century Christianity
e. Laodicean laxity of life _____

**18.** The term Paul uses to describe the new nature and the ability for holy living given to every Christian as part of his salvation is
a. the new man
b. the new birth
c. the new life
d. the new orthodoxy
e. the new and living way _____

**19.** The specific sin for which a believer may need cleansing and the specific virtue which may need enablement will
a. always correspond exactly with the needs of other Christians
b. vary greatly from one believer to another
c. depend on how far the believer has been successful in conquering evil habits in his own strength
d. only be revealed to that believer through prayer and fasting _____

**20.** The enablement for holy living is found in
a. ourselves
b. prayer
c. Christ
d. all the above _____

## WHAT DO YOU SAY?

To what extent are you obeying God? Give one example of a recent act of obedience in your life and its results.

_____

_____

_____

_____

_____

*MAIL TO address shown on back outside cover.*
*PLEASE enclose a stamped addressed envelope for the return of your corrected exam.*

# The Ascension in the Believer's Daily Life

## THE ASCENSION:
### Satan and the Need of Deliverance.

Standing between the Christian and a successful Christian life are not only his fallen nature and its enmity against God, and his innate lack of ability to do the will of God, but also his implacable foe—Satan.

The Christian has an enemy. To deny his existence, to underrate his power, and to be ignorant of his methods, or to fail to give heed to the Biblical warnings concerning Satan, can only result in spiritual loss.

The activity of Satan and his cunning counterfeits are disclosed in the Scriptures. He often comes as an "angel of light," in religious garb, to work with impunity among the children of God (2 Corinthians 11:13-15). So skilled is he in subterfuge and forgery that his activity is rarely recognized as evil. His influence is described as a "snare" (2 Timothy 2:26).

In a piercing exposé of the character and work of Satan, the Bible lists a number of descriptive titles; who he is, a fallen angel of great ability; and what he does, in his endeavor to strike out against God.

Satan is described as the believer's enemy through the title "Adversary" (1 Peter 5:8). This characterization of our foe is not to be taken lightly. Although it is true that the Christian belongs to God and is under His sovereign protection (Job 1:10), this does not mean the believer is automatically free from all Satanic influences. By a misunderstanding of spiritual truths or through disobedience to God, a

73

believer may permit such Satanic intervention in his life that he will suffer great spiritual anxiety and loss.

As an adversary, Satan has a clear-cut goal. He will endeavor in every way possible to keep the believer from any type of spiritual progress, enjoyment, or usefulness. If we cannot be enslaved through physical sins (Luke 4:33), the adversary too often succeeds by leading us to overemphasize some Biblical truth or practice until it becomes a sin (Acts 5:1-11; 2 Corinthians 2:10, 11; 11:13-15; 1 Timothy 3:6, 7). Every earnest Christian stands in great danger of such a spiritual perversion. This demonic activity is more prevalent in our churches today than we could imagine. As an angel of light, his ministry is almost beyond detection. Who would question the motivation of the legalist, the ascetic, the mystic, or the one caught up in unusual spiritual experiences? It would be plainly "unspiritual" to do so!

Our adversary works in the lives of Christians through temptation (1 Thessalonians 3:5). We have been frankly told that we will not be tempted by God (James 1:13). Although one is often tempted through his own fallen nature (James 1:14), these activities may also find their source in the Devil. Who does not face a constant barrage?

The activity of Satan is also described as a work of hindrance (1 Thessalonians 2:18). How often the serious Christian has experienced this influence in his life! It must be recognized that the paramount goal of our adversary is to thwart and inhibit the believer's spiritual progress. The genuine Christian will have hindrances placed in his path by Satan. This was true of the Apostle Paul as the above text indicates.

A third type of activity utilized by our adversary is that of deception (Revelation 12:9). With a heart that is deceitful (Jeremiah 17:9), the Christian is unusually vulnerable to this type of attack. In particular, Satan will endeavor to lead the believer into deception concerning spiritual truths and his own spiritual condition. The people of Judah, for example, were slowly led to believe that they were spiritual when they were not. Instead of loving God, they loved only religion. They were deceived. It was their religious deceit which finally brought their judgment and the Babylonian captivity (Jeremiah 7:1-16; 17:1-10). There are some things for which there is no cure—

religiousness is one of these (Jeremiah 2:22; 8:5; 9:6; 11:11, 14; 14:12).

The believer may not listen to his own religious feelings or conscience. If he does, he is opening the door to Satan. How *we* feel about our spiritual condition is never authoritative; all authority resides in God and is made known through His work in history and His Word. When we confuse the voice of God with our own voice, we open ourselves to demonic deception (Galatians 6:3; 2 Timothy 3:13; James 1:22, 26; 2 Peter 2:13).

Satan is also given the title of "Accuser" (Revelation 12:10). This designation characterizes one of the most serious and successful activities of our enemy. The Christian is not only accused before God (Job 1:9; Zechariah 3:1), he is led, by Satan, into a state of false self-condemnation.

To accomplish this insidious work the Devil adopts his "angel of light" subterfuge, and counterfeits the convicting work of the Holy Spirit. All serious Christians have been suddenly engulfed by an intense awareness of personal guilt. They are made to feel, by Satan, as though they had sinned and were, therefore, out of fellowship with God and under His condemnation.

Under such a demonic attack the Christian is soon rendered helpless. No amount of confession relieves the "conviction" of sin or the sense of estrangement. His joy disappears, he is thwarted in his attempt to do Christian service and, most serious of all, he is confused when his confession of sin does not result in forgiveness and restored fellowship.

In this situation the Christian who has discernment of the ways of the enemy will take spiritual stock. He will recognize the ambiguity and confusion which has characterized his "conviction." This will indicate to him that he has not been the recipient of the ministry of the Holy Spirit but has been under the accusation of the Devil.

When the Holy Spirit convicts of sin, His ministry is always characterized by clarity. The erring Christian is clearly shown *what* he has done wrong and *what he is to do about it.*

In direct contrast, the accusing work of Satan is always one of ambiguity. The Christian never knows what he has done or what he is to do to correct his situation. He is simply made to feel guilty and uneasy.

It is extremely important for the believer to learn this distinction between the ministry of the Holy Spirit and the counterfeiting of the Devil. As long as the believer accepts the accusations of Satan as true, his condition is hopeless. He must recognize what has happened, resist the Devil, and totally reject the accusations by a forthright decision of faith.

The titles of "Murderer" and "Liar" are also attributed to Satan (John 8:44). His objectives and actions in these areas are self-evident. His endeavors to take life and to pervert truth began in the Garden of Eden (1 Timothy 2:14) and will continue with the human race (1 John 3:12) until the final judgment (1 Timothy 4:1). We may not accept the demonic suggestion that our daily lives are without meaning and that self-destruction is the only "spiritual" alternative left. Nor may the believer allow himself to become the tool of Satan by accepting and repeating the insinuations and distortions of gossip. The Apostle Paul flatly stated that the person who is a gossip had been influenced by Satan (1 Timothy 5:13-15). It is important to recognize that of the seven things which God hates—the one who gossips has involved himself in six of these sins (Proverbs 6:16-19)!

The believer has an enemy and is in desperate need of deliverance.


## THE ASCENSION:
## Satan and the Provision of Deliverance.

The Lord Jesus Christ came into the world as man's Representative to defeat Satan and to deliver His people from all demonic influence. As the last Adam He triumphed victoriously in the very area where the first Adam had completely failed (Romans 5:12-19).

Under Satanic temptation, the incarnate Lord Jesus Christ not only corrected the demonic half-truths which were suggested to Him but also repulsed the enemy and commanded him to leave His presence (Matthew 4:1-11). It is important to understand that Jesus Christ took refuge in and employed the written Word of God.

In His daily ministry Christ's power over Satan was continually manifested. There was a constant recognition, on the part of demons, of Christ's divine Sonship, and of their total subjection to Him (Mark 3:11; 5:7; Luke 4:33-36).

The Apostle John boldly stated that the reason Jesus Christ came into the world was to destroy the works of Satan (1 John 3:8). The writer of Hebrews made a similar statement. He explained how the incarnation was necessary so that through His death, Christ could strip the Devil of his power (Hebrews 2:14) and deliver His people from Satan's bondage (Hebrews 2:15).

The Apostle Paul affirmed the atonement of Jesus Christ to be a public exposé of the defeat of Satan in which the Son of God triumphed gloriously (Colossians 2:15). Because of this victory over Satan it must be recognized that although the Christian has an insidious and implacable foe in the Devil—he is a defeated foe!

That which the Lord Jesus Christ obtained by His death He assumed and demonstrated in His ascension. The ascension, therefore, is filled with meaning for the believer. Christ has entered heaven, not only as Intercessor (Hebrews 4:14; 6:20; 7:25; 8:1; 9:11, 12) and the Head of the Church (Ephesians 1:22), to give gifts to His Church (Ephesians 4:8-11) and to bestow the Holy Spirit upon all believers (Acts 2:33), but also to rule over His enemies.

Jesus Christ was seated at the right hand of God in victory over Satan and all his forces of evil (Ephesians 1:19-23; 2:5, 6; Hebrews 1:13; 1 Peter 3:22). They were all placed "under His feet."

This deliverance and position of authority over Satan has been legally given to the believer. We have been made to "sit together in heavenly places in Christ Jesus" (Ephesians 2:6). Jesus Christ acted on our behalf as our Representative. As a "joint-heir" with Christ we share in His victory (Romans 8:17; Ephesians 6:16).


## THE ASCENSION:
### Satan and the Provisions of Deliverance.

In his salvation, the believer was delivered from the kingdom and power of Satan and brought into the kingdom of God (Acts 26:18; Colossians 1:13). He, therefore, no longer lives under the dominion of the god of this world (Ephesians 2:1-3; 2 Corinthians 4:4). He has been set free.

However, it is one thing to be free from Satan in the area of salvation and quite another to maintain that freedom in the area of sanctification. The believer, through divine grace in salvation, now belongs to Jesus Christ. Therefore, he will never again belong to Satan. This does not mean, however, that Satan cannot make the believer's life miserable and ineffectual.

The Christian has been exhorted to resist the Devil (James 4:7; 1 Peter 5:8). This simply means to refuse to accept, or act in harmony with, the insinuations, accusations, or temptations of the enemy. The Apostle Paul was right in warning us that this takes sobriety, vigilance, and steadfastness (1 Peter 5:8, 9).

Except for unusual situations, as those described in the book of Job, the only way Satan can influence the Christian is through some aspect of sinfulness. This is what the Apostle Paul was referring to when he warned the Ephesian Christians, "Neither give place to the Devil" (Ephesians 4:27). When the believer allows the Devil a "place" or "foothold" in his life, the Devil will exploit that opportunity to the fullest.

There are at least four illustrations in the New Testament of giving opportunity to Satan. Two of these illustrations have to do with the pastoral office and two with the membership in the church.

The Apostle Paul warned Timothy that the elder may not be a novice and that he must have a good report among those who are not Christians. A novice would be almost certain to become proud, and if one did not have a good report he would not only be open to criticism but would be tempted to be hypocritical. These, Paul stated, would make the elder vulnerable to the condemnation and snare of the Devil (1 Timothy 3:6, 7). Pride, inconsistency, and hypocrisy have caused the fall of many. They leave the Christian defenseless.

The third illustration has to do with forgiveness among church members. The church at Corinth had disciplined one of its members for immorality and was now exhorted to receive him back, since he had repented. Paul wrote to the church and warned them to forgive the man and to love him. Not to do so would have presented to Satan an "advantage" (2 Corinthians 2:1-11).

Many Christians and churches have failed to obey this exhortation. Not only have the people displayed a lack of forgiveness but they have added the sin of gossip. To make the situation worse, many repentant believers have not found love upon returning to their church but, instead, a cold stony indifference. Satan had been given the "advantage."

The fourth illustration describes two church members. Ananias and Sapphira pretended to be more spiritual than they were. Their profession did not match their inner walk with God. They had accepted a suggestion of Satan and had put it into practice. Their judgment serves as a warning to all hypocrites (Acts 5:1-11).

Any failure to obey God opens the door to Satanic influence. When the Christian chooses to disobey God, he is acting as did Eve in the Garden. Eve allowed Satan to question the authority of God's Word and accepted his demonic interpretation. Having done this, it was quite easy for her to put the insinuations into practice. When the believer chooses to sin, he is acting, as did Eve, on the premise that the Word of God is not final authority. By failing to obey God we not only destroy our spirituality, but we allow Satan to ensnare us (2 Timothy 2:25, 26).

To escape this tragic situation and its inexorable result we must learn to obey God and "resist the Devil." In response to Satanic questioning of the Word of God and deceptive insinuations concerning the will of God, we must steadfastly affirm the truthfulness of the Word and will of God (1 Peter 5:8, 9; Matthew 4:1-11).

In obeying the exhortation to resist the Devil, the Apostle Paul stated that the most important factor was understanding and using the "shield of faith" (Ephesians 6:16). This we are to do "above all." The shield is more valuable than any of the other items of the Christian's armor (Ephesians 6:11-18). This "shield" is a symbolic representation of a believer's decision of faith, which will successfully thwart the attacks of Satan. The Apostle Peter stated the same truth (1 Peter 5:9).

The faith to which both Peter and Paul were referring is the believer's wholehearted trust in, and commitment to, Jesus Christ and His successful triumph over Satan. This faith is the decision to stand in the value of, and to appropriate the power of, Christ's victory. The Christian has every right to do this since the power of Christ's work has been imputed to him. When we make the decision to obey God fully, to trust in the Person and work of Jesus Christ, and to live accordingly, we will learn what it means to resist the Devil, and we will have the ability to do so. We will have a "shield of faith."

These exhortations are summarized in the book of Revelation in the description of the overcomers (Revelation 12:11). The secret of their victory over Satan was three-fold. The reference to "the blood of the Lamb," indicates the victorious triumph of Jesus Christ in whom they trusted. "The word of their testimony," refers to their decisions of faith to appropriate Christ's victory. And, finally, the statement, "they loved not their lives unto the death," portrays their committal to Jesus Christ even though it meant death.

For too many Christians this description of life is entirely foreign to their own daily existence. The problem is not with the provision of God nor with the Biblical exhortations. The reason many Christians do not experience deliverance or even feel the need of divine help is because of their attitude: *they couldn't care less!* With that kind of attitude about spiritual things the average Christian will very likely not be bothered by Satanic influences. He has made his own life ineffectual!

When you have mastered this lesson, take the first part of Exam 5 (covering lesson 8), questions 1-10 on pages 93-95 (right after lesson 9). Remember you will not turn this exam in for correction until after you have done lesson 9.

# Pentecost in the Believer's Daily Life

**PENTECOST:**
**The Promise of the Holy Spirit in the Old Testament.**

Theologically speaking, everything that has been said up to this point is purely theory. Only with the ministry of the Holy Spirit may one legitimately speak of daily practice. God the Holy Spirit has come to *apply* the provision the Lord Jesus Christ has obtained for the believer. Through His work of the new birth, the Christian has been transformed; and through His work of anointing, the believer is enabled to live the Christian life successfully.

One of the most encouraging and impressive promises of the Old Testament has to do with the Holy Spirit. It is found in Joel 2:28, 29. There God promises that the day will come when He will pour out His Spirit equally upon all His people. In that day it will not make a difference if one is a man or a woman, old or young, master or servant. All will receive the Holy Spirit alike.

This does not mean that the Old Testament saints were without the ministry of the Holy Spirit. When Jesus Christ said to Nicodemus that a person must be born of the Spirit to enter the kingdom of God, His stipulation applied equally well to all people in all of time (John 3:3, 5). It is evident that the Old Testament saints were recipients of the ministry of the Holy Spirit in the new birth, in that they are used as an illustration of salvation to New Testament saints. According to the writer of Hebrews, salvation by faith was true of Abel (Hebrews

11:4). David (Romans 4:6), Abraham (Romans 4:10-25; Galatians 3:6-14), and Rahab (James 2:25, 26) are similar examples.

It must be recognized that there was also an anointing of certain individuals in the Old Testament by the Holy Spirit. Bezaleel and Aholiab were anointed to enable them to build the tabernacle (Exodus 35:30-35). And there was the anointing of Saul (1 Samuel 10:10) and David (1 Samuel 16:13) as kings over Israel. Moses (Numbers 11:25) and Joshua (Numbers 27:18) were anointed to lead the children of Israel. The various judges were anointed to deliver the people of God from their enemies (Judges 3:10; 6:34, etc.). The Holy Spirit came upon the prophets to inspire them to speak forth the message given to them by God (1 Chronicles 12:18; 2 Chronicles 15:1; 20:14; 24:20). Even upon Balaam, a false prophet, God placed His Spirit so the demonic endeavors of Balak would be thwarted (Numbers 24:2).

## PENTECOST:
### The Promise of the Holy Spirit in the New Testament.

As great as this ministry was in Old Testament times, God promised through Joel that a day would come when it would be transcended. This theme was taken up by the last of the Old Testament prophets and further explained. John the Baptist stated that the Holy Spirit would be given by the Messiah (John 1:33). This clarifying statement is of great importance. It determines the theological perspective for all that the New Testament states concerning the Holy Spirit, in that the ministry of the Spirit would always be inseparably related to the Person of the Lord Jesus and the carrying out of His purpose.

Additional clarification concerning the ministry of the Holy Spirit was given by the Lord Jesus Christ Himself. There are five passages in the New Testament in which the coming of the Holy Spirit is further clarified.

The first is in John 7:37-39. Jesus Christ stated that all those who would thirst, who would come to Him and drink, believing on Him, would themselves become the source of living water. The Apostle John observed that this invitation and promise revolved around the coming of the Holy Spirit who had not yet been given.

In this passage there are two factors of importance which have been pointed out previously. The first has to do with how one receives the Holy Spirit. This, we are told, is by believing on the Lord Jesus Christ. The second has to do with the result of His ministry in our lives. We will become the means of life-giving help to other people. These words of the Lord Jesus boldly cut through the worry and uncertainty so characteristic of many Christians. Here is the answer to the doubt and uncertainty which revolve around the question of personal ability to live a meaningful life.

What is His answer to our weakness in life and service? He states that we must thirst for Him, come to Him, and drink of Him in faith. As always, the problem is not in the *provision,* but in the lack of *appropriation.* When we learn how to respond by faith and thereby give Jesus Christ His rightful place, there will be a spontaneous ministry of the Holy Spirit to us and through us. Faith and love must be more than verbal pronouncements; they must be activities of life. That which determines our relationship to the Holy Spirit is our relationship to Jesus Christ.

The second passage of clarification is found in John 14:16-20. Here the Lord Jesus characterizes the Person and work of the Holy Spirit in ascribing two titles to Him. The first is "Comforter" which means in the original language, "One called alongside." By this title we are taught that the Holy Spirit would be a constant help to the believer, as one called to his aid, by standing alongside. It is significant that the Lord Jesus also stated the Holy Spirit would be "another Comforter." He was, therefore, to take the place of Christ Himself with His disciples. The significance of this truth is almost beyond human comprehension. That God Himself, the Holy Spirit, would come to us to be our Helper, is overwhelming!

The second title of the Holy Spirit is that of "Spirit of Truth." This indicates the purpose of His coming. He is the divine Teacher of truth. Because non-Christians reject the truth and love darkness rather than light (John 3:19), they cannot receive nor will they receive this ministry of the Spirit. However the Holy Spirit has come to every believer—to be his Teacher (1 John 2:20, 27).

In application of these two titles, the Lord Jesus explained how He would come to the disciples in the coming of the Holy Spirit (John 14:18); and that they would become the recipients of assurance and illumination (John 14:19, 20). The same promise is summarized later in the chapter (John 14:25, 26).

A third passage of instruction in this farewell discourse is found in John 15:26, 27. The titles of the Holy Spirit are restated as well as the emphasis on the relationship of His ministry to that of the Lord Jesus and to God the Father. The additional element here is on the purpose of His coming. The Lord Jesus said, "He shall testify of Me, and ye also shall bear witness. . . ." The Holy Spirit would comfort, instruct, and illuminate those who believe on the Lord Jesus so that they may be enabled, through His indwelling presence, to bear witness themselves.

The fourth section of importance concerning the ministry of the Holy Spirit is found in John 16:7-16. Here we are told that the Holy Spirit will convict the non-Christian of sin, righteousness, and of a future judgment. All mankind are the recipients of this reproof.

In addition to what has been said in the previous passages, about the work of the Holy Spirit in the believer, this passage includes two further statements of great importance. The first is found in verse 13, ". . . He shall not speak of Himself. . . ." This really means that the Holy Spirit does not speak independently of the Father and the Son. The ministry of the Spirit is generally away from Himself to Christ. All endeavors, whether by the individual Christian or by a church or denomination, to place the Holy Spirit at the center of their attention and instruction is, therefore, suspect.

The second statement clearly expresses the purpose of the Holy Spirit's ministry. It is found in verse 14. The Lord Jesus said, "He shall glorify Me. . . ." Instead of drawing attention to Himself, the Holy Spirit would magnify Jesus Christ. This is His goal in the life of the individual believer and in the ministry of the church. *Jesus Christ is to be given His rightful place at the center of all things.* When the believer or church chooses to do this, then there is a cooperation with the Holy Spirit and the result can only be spiritual success. When this is not done, weakness will inevitably follow. The importance of these truths can hardly be overemphasized.

The fifth passage of explanation is found in Acts 1:4, 5, 8. The Lord Jesus, after His resurrection from the grave, instructed His followers to wait in Jerusalem for the fulfillment of the promises concerning the Holy Spirit. They were to be baptized with the Spirit and would thereby receive the power or ability to be witnesses for Jesus Christ throughout the whole world.

## PENTECOST:
### The Manifestation of the Holy Spirit.

Fifty days after the resurrection of the Lord Jesus, the Old Testament and New Testament promises regarding the coming of the Holy Spirit were fulfilled. In obedience to the instruction of the Lord Jesus (Acts 1:4, 5, 8), a group of His disciples were praying together when the Holy Spirit descended upon them. With the sound of a great wind and with the appearance of fire, the Holy Spirit filled all the disciples (Acts 2:1-4).

As a further demonstration of the presence of the Holy Spirit, all the disciples began to speak with tongues so that the many strangers in Jerusalem heard the gospel preached in their own language. As a result three thousand persons responded to the commands and promise of the gospel and were baptized (Acts 2:4-11, 37-47).

The Apostle Peter that same day explained the meaning of this great event. He quoted the promise concerning the Holy Spirit as given in Joel 2:28, 29 and indicated that it had now been fulfilled (Acts 2:14ff). The coming of the Holy Spirit, Peter expounded, was due to the activity of the ascended Lord Jesus who had poured out the Spirit upon His people (Acts 2:33). Pentecost, therefore, was further and conclusive evidence of the resurrection and exaltation of the Lord Jesus Christ as the Son of God (Acts 2:29-36).

It is important to understand that Pentecost, like the crucifixion, resurrection, and ascension, happened only once. It is also important to see that the Church, now called the Body of Christ (Ephesians 1:22, 23), was brought into existence in this outpouring of the Holy Spirit.

Before this time the Church is spoken of as yet in the future (Matthew 16:18). But now on the day of Pentecost the Church is described as present (Acts 2:47), and continually referred to from this time forward.

The spiritual value of these two truths is of great significance to the believer. Today, when an individual repents of sin and receives Jesus Christ as Savior and Lord, he is baptized by the Holy Spirit into the Church (1 Corinthians 12:13). By this great act, the believer becomes a member of the Church and receives all the benefits of the day of Pentecost.

The Holy Spirit has come! The promises have been fulfilled. The Body of Christ has been brought into existence and is made up of people baptized with the Holy Spirit. To become a Christian means one is added to that baptized group and in turn receives all the spiritual benefits the first disciples received on the day of Pentecost (1 Corinthians 12:13-27).

In order to avoid confusion, it is necessary to distinguish between the spiritual benefits of Pentecost and the public demonstration of that day. The public display of power in the wind, the fire, and the speaking with tongues were given by God to indicate the importance and significance of that great event. The wind and fire would immediately call to mind the supernatural activity of God with the prophets (1 Kings 18:38; 19:11, 12; Ezekiel 1:4; etc.), and the speaking in tongues was a public evidence that the promise of Joel concerning an anointing of *all* of God's people had indeed come to pass. Such a manifestation of power also characterized the crucifixion, resurrection, and ascension. The Christian now possesses the legal benefits of all of these great deeds of God. It would be as wrong for one to expect the wind, fire, and tongues of the day of Pentecost to characterize his relationship with God today as to expect the darkness of the crucifixion, the earthquake of the resurrection, or the appearance of angels of the ascension.

What are the benefits of the day of Pentecost which all believers now possess? The Scripture describes this great provision of God under five headings. The first we have already considered. It is that of baptism with the Holy Spirit whereby one is brought into a saving relationship with the Lord Jesus Christ and made a member of the Church which is His Body (1 Corinthians 12:13). When does this happen? This important event happens the moment one believes on Jesus Christ as Savior and Lord. In fact, all of these five benefits come to pass at exactly the same time.

The second benefit of the day of Pentecost is described as the new birth (John 3:3, 5). In this act of the Holy Spirit the repentant and believing sinner is given the spiritual life obtained for him by Jesus Christ in His atonement (John 10:10; 1 John 5:9-13). This benefit, of course, was not new. Old Testament believers were thus quickened (John 3:10).

The third benefit is that of being indwelt by the Holy Spirit. The believer thereby becomes the temple of the Holy Spirit (1 Corinthians 3:16, 17; 6:19; 2 Corinthians 6:16).

The fourth benefit is described as being sealed with the Holy Spirit (2 Corinthians 1:22; Ephesians 1:13, 14; 4:30). The term "seal" is taken from the practice of "sealing" a legal document with a bit of wax into which an official "seal" or stamp was pressed. The emphasis here is upon the truth of ownership. The believer, by this act of the Holy Spirit, is shown to belong to God. Another work of the Holy Spirit is described as the "earnest." He pledges that all the future benefits of redemption will also be given the believer (2 Corinthians 1:22; 5:5; Ephesians 1:14).

The fifth benefit is the bestowal of gifts by the Holy Spirit. Every Christian has been given some ability or talent so that he can make a meaningful contribution to the furtherance of God's plan. In this regard it is important to see that the Apostle Paul described the Church by the analogy of the human body. As every member of the body must contribute to the full expression of the person, so every member of the Church has been given a gift and this gift must be utilized so that the Church may express itself fully (1 Corinthians 12:4-31; Ephesians 4:7-16). This is God's provision not only for the individual believer but also for the furtherance of the local church. When God's people are spiritually alert and exercising their divine gifts, the individual church will find itself adequately staffed with workers.

These benefits appear to be included in the Scripture under the term "anointing" (2 Corinthians 1:21; 1 John 2:20, 27). The Christian is, therefore, spoken of as one who has been anointed by the Holy

Spirit. This again points back to the ministry of the Holy Spirit in the Old Testament. The New Testament emphasis is also indicated in that *all* the believers now receive this anointing alike. And all have received the five great benefits of Pentecost.

But now we must face a practical question of spiritual importance. If all believers possess these benefits of Pentecost, why are these benefits not more enjoyed and utilized? What a tremendous thing it is to be baptized, born again, indwelt, sealed, and gifted by the Holy Spirit! How dare we be filled with uncertainty and weakness?

The answer is clear and yet hard to confess. The *fact* of these great benefits depends on the work of God within us. The resultant assurance, power, and enjoyment of these benefits depends upon us. It is one thing to possess this provision of Pentecost—and quite another to know how to live, and then to so live, that this divine provision may be adequately manifested in our daily lives.

## PENTECOST:
### The Ministry of the Holy Spirit.

We have been commanded by God to "be filled with the Holy Spirit" (Ephesians 5:18). The Christian has no vote in this matter. Living a Spirit-filled life is not optional. And to choose to disobey God condemns one to a life largely devoid of divine fellowship, grace, love, and purpose.

What does it mean to be filled with the Holy Spirit? It means, in all simplicity, to be surrendered to God (Romans 12:1, 2) so that the Holy Spirit can do in and through us what He was sent to do. Endless numbers of books have been written explaining this one profound truth. Have so many words confused us?

The Christian is seriously warned against hindering this ministry of the Holy Spirit in his life. Ananias and Sapphira are held up as an example of *lying to* (deceiving) or *tempting* the Holy Spirit (Acts 5:3, 9). Stephen accused those who refused the truth of the Word of God of *resisting* the Holy Spirit (Acts 7:51). The Apostle Paul stated that the believer who is unconcerned and slothful about putting the Word of God into daily practice, is *grieving* the Holy Spirit (Ephesians 4:30). And those Christians who scorn and deride the expression of the Holy Spirit in their own lives and the lives of others are *quenching* the Holy Spirit (1 Thessalonians 5:19).

These four sins clearly and tragically describe what it means to practice a lack of surrender to God. They vividly indicate the anti-surrender which characterizes the lives of most Christians. How easy it is to practice these four sins by substituting pretense for honesty, doubt for faith, disobedience for obedience, and an attitude of scornful self-complacency for one of grateful desire for every manifestation of the Holy Spirit.

And now we know why we are not Spirit filled! We lie to, resist, grieve, and quench the Holy Spirit! The lethargic unconcern manifested by many Christians about this indisputable truth only proves the correctness of this accusation.

What must we do to live a genuine Christian life and be filled with the Spirit? First of all, we must stop blaming God for being spiritually empty (Jeremiah 2:5, 13). In a close connection with this, we must stop contriving theological reasons for our lack and thereby turn our faults into virtues! God is not to blame. The Holy Spirit has come— there is no need to wait for Him. Ever since the day of Pentecost, which happened only once, every believer has had all the value and provision of Pentecost given to him in his salvation (Romans 8:9). *We* are at fault.

Secondly, we must confess our sins and stop committing them. We must stop pretending—stop acting as though we hadn't sinned, acting as though we are right with God. We must stop resisting the Holy Spirit—stop being so irresponsible about truth and our personal progress with God. We must stop grieving the Holy Spirit—stop being so unconcerned about putting the Word of God into practice. We must stop quenching the Holy Spirit—stop scoffing at those who are our examples in spirituality and start thirsting for God ourselves.

Thirdly, we must thoroughly understand why the Holy Spirit indwells us and learn how to cooperate with Him. He was sent to achieve clearly defined goals in our lives. These goals we must make our own by deliberate decisions of faith and practice.

The first goal the Holy Spirit has been commissioned to fulfill is that of glorifying Jesus Christ *in* the believer. Before the Christian can practice honesty he must *become* a holy person. Before he can practice love, joy, peace, etc., (the fruit of the Spirit, Galatians 5:22, 23), he must *experience* love, joy, peace. The Holy Spirit has been sent to take the word of Jesus Christ in His crucifixion, resurrection, and ascension and make personal application of this cleansing, enablement, and deliverance in the very character of the believer. This is what sanctification is all about. This is how the Holy Spirit leads and teaches the believer to mortify (put to death) the sinful attitudes and practices of the old nature (Romans 8:1-13) and to experience the freedom of sonship (Romans 8:14-17).

We are, therefore, to "walk (live) in the Spirit" (Galatians 5:16). When this is done there will be a freedom, a deliverance from the overpowering desires of the old nature (Galatians 5:16). Without this cooperation, a deadening, discouraging tension is set up in our lives (Galatians 5:17), and we live without a sense of purpose and progress and without love and joy and peace.

The Holy Spirit has thus been sent to enable us to give Jesus Christ His rightful place at the center of our lives. We must learn how to give Him that place as our Lord, our sanctification, as the Head of the Church, as the Lord of the harvest field, and as the living Word.

How tragically different is the Biblical description of the Spirit-filled life from what we often see in our own lives! Many Christians have earnestly tried to *practice* the Christian life without realizing that the real need was *within.* As a result the practice was partially a pretense and the vicious cycle started again.

The second goal the Holy Spirit has been sent to achieve is that of glorifying the Lord Jesus Christ *through* the believer (John 15:26, 27). The emphasis here is on daily practice and witnessing. The Lord Jesus often spoke of this as a spontaneous result of the indwelling Holy Spirit (John 7:37-39; 15:26, 27; Acts 1:8). When the believer cooperates with the Holy Spirit in regard to the first goal of personal sanctification, this second goal will be achieved automatically. The believer will then be, in character, a witness, and he will not find it difficult to speak up for his Lord. This is a self-condemning explanation of our lack of faithful witnessing.

What determines our daily relationship to the Holy Spirit? What does it mean, and how are we to be filled? We must be taken up with the Lord Jesus Christ! We must respond to Him and His Word by faith and love and thereby give Him His rightful place in our lives. We must learn to live in fellowship with God and in daily obedience. The Holy Spirit has been sent to glorify Jesus Christ in our lives, and when we give Him His rightful place, then we are filled with the Holy Spirit. This is why the Holy Spirit is called, "the Spirit of Christ" (Romans 8:9).

When you are ready, complete Exam 5 by answering questions 11-20 on pages 95-97. (You should have already answered questions 1-10 as part of your study of lesson 8.)

When you have answered all the questions in Exam 5, mail the exam for correction.

# HIGHER GROUND

Name_____  Exam Grade_____
(print plainly)

Address _____

City_____ State _____ Zip Code _____ Class Number _____

Instructor _____

## LESSON 8

*In the blank space in the right-hand margin write the letter of the correct answer.*

1. In which of the following guises does Satan seek to subvert the work of God in a *religious* way? When he comes as
   a. the old serpent
   b. an angel of light
   c. a great red dragon
   d. a roaring lion                                              _____

2. As the believer's Adversary, Satan's goal is to
   a. deprive the believer of his salvation
   b. dazzle the believer by appearing before him in shining splendor as an angel
   c. destroy the believer's usefulness to God and rob the believer of his joy
   d. do all the above                                           _____

3. Satan is a Deceiver. He
   a. deceives the unsaved but cannot deceive the believer for the believer is indwelt by the Holy Spirit
   b. deceived the Israelites, but cannot deceive the Christian for "we are not ignorant of his devices"
   c. deceives himself into thinking he can deceive Christians, "the saints of the Most High"
   d. can and does deceive believers concerning what the Bible teaches

4. A Christian feels he has sinned against God and has deep feelings of conviction. He finds it difficult to discern exactly how or where he has grieved the Holy Spirit. He confesses his sin again and again to God but still feels estranged and unhappy. He should
   a. recognize that he is being deceived by Satan and reject the accusations
   b. keep on confessing his sins to the Lord until he finds the relief he seeks
   c. forget the whole thing and continue serving the Lord as though nothing were wrong
   d. face the fact that he has committed the unpardonable sin    _____

5. Which of the following, particularly described in Proverbs 6: 16-19, is a snare of Satan for the soul?
   a. Cruelty
   b. Filthy-mindedness
   c. Hypocrisy
   d. Gossip    _____

6. When tempted by the Devil, the Lord Jesus
   a. sought refuge in His essential Deity which was incapable of being tempted
   b. fell back on the written Word of God
   c. fled from the temptation so that it lost its power of appeal
   d. performed a miracle to prove He was the Son of God and thus beyond Satan's reach    _____

7. Which of the following aspects of Christ's ascension apply to all believers with special significance? He
   a. has entered heaven as our Intercessor
   b. is Head of the body, the Church, and bestows gifts upon it
   c. gives the Holy Spirit to all believers
   d. rules over all His foes
   e. has done all the above and sits the believer with Himself in heavenly places    _____

8. When James told believers to "resist the Devil and he will flee from you" he prefaced the injunction with the words—
   a. "if so be the Spirit of Christ dwell in you"
   b. "submit yourselves unto God"
   c. "walk in the light as He (God) is in the light"
   d. "neither give place to the Devil"    _____

9. A believer gives place to the Devil when he
   a. is confronted by a personal manifestation of the Devil and flees in terror
   b. tolerates some known sin in his life
   c. feels very strongly about a particular doctrine, which he has studied to the exclusion of balancing truth, and then, realizing that his viewpoint will cause friction with his brethren, refuses to actively promote it
   d. insists that an erring brother be disciplined by the church _____

10. Which of the following was characteristic of the victorious believers mentioned in Revelation 12. They
    a. claimed the power of Christ's victory at Calvary
    b. took positive steps to appropriate Christ's victory
    c. were committed, without reservations, to a life of victory
    d. were victorious because they manifested all the above characteristics
    e. were victorious because they had been baptized by the Holy Spirit into the body of Christ _____

## WHAT DO YOU SAY?

How has this lesson particularly helped you?

_____

_____

_____

_____

_____

# LESSON 9

*In the blank space in the right-hand margin write the letter of the correct answer.*

11. The possibility of the new birth
    a. was first extended to Nicodemus
    b. is exclusively a characteristic of the New Testament believer in contrast with the Old Testament believer who was saved by faith apart from the new birth
    c. was extended to men in Old Testament times just as much as in New Testament times
    d. extends only to Jews _____

95

**12.** It is evident from Scripture that in the Old Testament
- a. there was an anointing of the Spirit for service as distinct from the usual work of the Spirit
- b. the anointing of the Spirit took the place of what we would call today the regeneration of the Spirit (i.e. the new birth)
- c. only those who were devout and instructed believers in God possessed of pure motives and holy desires were anointed by the Spirit
- d. the anointing of the Spirit was reserved for prophets, priests and kings _____

**13.** True Christians are to be channels through which flows the Holy Spirit in outpoured blessing to others. We receive the Spirit in this way
- a. only after a prolonged period of wrestling with God in prayer
- b. by believing in the Lord Jesus Christ
- c. as a result of the Holy Spirit's having persistently drawn attention to Himself
- d. when we speak in tongues as the disciples did at Pentecost since "tongues" is the great evidence that a believer is empowered for service _____

**14.** The great function of the Holy Spirit as "the Comforter" is to
- a. console the believer for losses and hardships suffered as he lives the Christian life
- b. bring comfort to the heart of God in the assurance that His work on earth is in the capable hands of the Holy Spirit
- c. come alongside the believer as his Helper and particularly to help the believer grasp and apply Divine truth
- d. convict the world, which crucified the Lord Jesus, of sin, righteousness and judgment _____

**15.** The Spirit's great work is to GLORIFY the Lord Jesus. We are specifically told this in
- a. John 7:37-39
- b. John 14:16-20
- c. John 15:26, 27
- d. John 16:13, 14
- e. 1 John 2:20, 27
- f. Acts 1:4 _____

16. The BAPTISM of the Holy Spirit is that ministry of the Holy Spirit which
    a. enables all believers who experience it to speak in tongues
    b. takes place subsequent to conversion as a "second work of grace" or a "second blessing"
    c. is repetitive in the believer's experience and may be summed up thus—"One filling; many baptisms"
    d. makes a believer a member of the Church, the mystical body of Christ                                                    _____

17. The SEAL of the Spirit
    a. sets the believer's body apart as God's temple
    b. guarantees that the believer belongs to God
    c. imparts to the believer spiritual gifts to be used in evangelizing the lost and edifying the Church
    d. provides continuity between the Old Testament ministry of the Spirit and the New Testament ministry of the Spirit     _____

18. The FILLING of the Spirit
    a. makes it possible for God to put into practical effect in our lives all the things for which He has given us His Spirit
    b. may be described as conditional but not optional
    c. hinges on the believer's surrender of himself to God
    d. embraces all the above facts                                                                                          _____

19. In order to be filled with the Spirit we must
    a. wait (i.e. "tarry") in God's presence for an extended period of time as the disciples did just prior to Pentecost
    b. confess our sins and stop resisting the Holy Spirit
    c. first live lives which are free from sin altogether
    d. enter into some form of full-time Christian service                                                                   _____

20. How can a believer know as a daily, living reality in his life the cleansing, enablement and deliverance wrought for him by the Lord Jesus in His crucifixion, resurrection and ascension?
    a. He must try his hardest to live a good, fruitful Christian life
    b. He cannot know these things in his life this side of heaven because he has an inbred tendency to sin
    c. He can achieve these things only after he becomes a mature believer with years of experience in living the Christian life behind him
    d. The Holy Spirit has been sent to make these things true in the experience of each child of God                        _____

## WHAT DO YOU SAY?

Are you filled with the Spirit? How do you know?

_____

_____

_____

_____

_____

*MAIL TO address shown on back outside cover.*
*PLEASE enclose a stamped addressed envelope for the return of your corrected exam.*

# "And Now Faith Is..."

## THE BIBLICAL DEMAND:
## Only Faith will do!

It is one thing to know the truth but it is quite another to put the truth into practice. The desire to be a successful Christian is not enough. Nor is it sufficient to give an intellectual assent to the Scripture. The Biblical demand is quite clear—only faith will do! "... Without faith it is *impossible* to please Him ..." (Hebrews 11:6).

Therefore, the issue is not this or that sin; it is not our money, nor our talent, nor our time, nor our work, nor is it even the various doctrines we accept. The issue is not our prayer life and its length; it is not our service for Christ and its amount; it is not our church attendance and its frequency; it is not our Bible study and its depth; it is not our sincerity and its transparency—the issue is *faith*.

What is this necessary ingredient which acts as a catalyst between knowledge and practice? What is it that God demands of me?

Faith will never be understood as long as it is considered to be, and investigated as, an abstract idea or an isolated virtue. Faith is inseparably related to genuine Christianity. While the term may be used in a great variety of ways, such as putting one's faith in a person, an instrument, or a medicine, in the Biblical sense faith is much more strictly defined. It is not enough to say that the person who believes in a false religion has faith. Of course he has faith, but it is condemned by the Bible as false. The Biblical Christian and the Buddhist both have faith, but the faith of the former is true and the faith of the latter is spurious in the sense that it has a false object even though his sincerity may be beyond reproach.

Biblical Christianity revolves around the Person of Jesus Christ. Therefore, Biblical faith is inseparably related to correct belief and action regarding Jesus Christ.

Biblical Christianity is rooted in the redemptive work of Jesus Christ in history. Therefore, Biblical faith is inseparably related to correct belief and action regarding the atonement.

Biblical Christianity is based upon the revelation of God in the Scriptures. Therefore, Biblical faith is inseparably related to correct belief and action regarding the Bible.

Perhaps at this point it would be helpful to ask about a definition of Biblical faith. While there are many facets to faith, a definition would include at least the following points:

Faith is the response of the total person to God as a Person in loving submission, trust, and obedience; in and through the Person of Jesus Christ as the revelation of God and Redeemer of mankind, who as the sovereign Lord offers Himself to the believer, through the ministry of the Holy Spirit and the Scriptures, as his daily sufficiency.


## THE BIBLICAL EXPLANATION (1):
## Faith is a Decision to Respond Correctly to God.

Faith is not feeling—but a *decision*. This is what is meant by the word "response" in the above definition. Faith is, therefore, a correct response to God. Unbelief and doubt are the opposite of faith. They are incorrect responses to God.

God has revealed Himself. What we choose to do with Him and His Word is very important. When we make a choice to obey the commandments of God and to claim His promises, we have made a decision. It is a correct response to the God of the Word. It is faith. When we choose to disobey God through His commandments and to reject His promises, we have also made a decision, but it is an incorrect response to the God of the Word. It is doubt and unbelief.

In Hebrews 11 we are given a series of illustrations of faith. A number of individuals are described in many circumstances of life, all making a decision to respond harmoniously to God and His Word. Moses is a good example of such decision-making. In verses 24-28 there are five words which illustrate his response to God. These words are "refused," "choosing," "esteeming," "forsook," and "kept." Each indicates a decision on the part of Moses. God has revealed His will to Moses: he was not to stay in Egypt; he was to lead the Israelites into Canaan. These five words indicate how he responded to God by making the right decisions to obey God's Word. This is what the Bible means by "faith."

How the Christian feels about his faith and ability to live by faith has nothing to do with it. The all-important factor is his choice and decision.

Faith has three very clear characteristics. The first is that of *submission to God and His Word.* Without this necessary ingredient it is ridiculous for us to think we can make a correct decision of faith. Any lack of concern for the will of God and all decisions to disobey the Word of God not only bring a disruption of fellowship in the life of the Christian but make a decision of faith, in the area of his insubordination, impossible.

The second characteristic of faith is the *practice of obedience.* Genuine faith is a correct response to God and this is always inseparable from obedience in daily life. This is one reason why it is so difficult for us to live by faith when we do not wish to obey God. It is absurd for us to try to exercise faith about a matter when we are apathetic about obeying God or when we have made the decision not to obey! This is part of the theme of Hebrews 11. Each illustration of faith in that chapter is also an illustration of obedience. Faith is not primarily a sense of dependency on God. It is a decision to submit to God through His Word and to put the Word of God into daily practice.

The third characteristic of faith is that of *trust.* This is also a necessary ingredient for Biblical faith. It is the inseparable companion to submission and the practice of obedience. When Moses made the decision to submit to the directive of God to lead the Israelites out of

Egypt, and sought to obey God, he did so in trust. He trusted God to give him wisdom and strength to obey and also trusted God to make the journey possible. At the very least, this trust involved making the Israelites willing to go, dealing with Pharaoh and his armies, opening the Red Sea, and supplying food and water.

God expects us to trust Him. When we choose to obey His Word, and put that choice into daily obedience, God pledges Himself to make His will possible. Abraham expressed this trust in the words, "And being fully persuaded that, what He had promised, He was able also to perform" (Romans 4:21). This third characteristic of faith was also expressed by Paul. During the storm at sea he said, "Wherefore, sirs, be of good cheer: for I believe God, that it shall be even as it was told me" (Acts 27:25).

God is worthy of our trust. He is the truth. What He has promised He will fulfill and what He has commanded He will make possible.


## THE BIBLICAL EXPLANATION (2):
Faith has a Person as its Object—God.

Biblical faith is not to be confused with personal self-confidence, nor is it a trust in the goodness of man. We have not been told to put faith in the Church, nor in a group of religious ideas. We are to trust God.

Only God is the object of Biblical faith. In the hour of the disciples' greatest need, the Lord Jesus simply asked them to trust *Him* (John 14:1). The message of the Bible is unmistakable on this point. "Abraham believed *God* . . ." (Romans 4:3). "Have faith in *God*" (Mark 11:22). It was the Lord Jesus who said, "And if I say the truth, why do ye not believe *Me?*" (John 8:46).

This simple truth can be an immeasurable help in the Christian life. Faith is not blind. It is not an ambiguous trust in some abstract entity. It is not a leap in the dark. *God* is the object of faith. Because of His revelation, God and His will can be known and acted upon (John 17:3). There may be times when God will ask us to trust Him without the benefit of inner assurance or compatible circumstances. This, undoubtedly, was true of Job (Job 13:15) and Abraham (Romans 4:16-21). But even this is not "blind faith." These men believed God and His Word, in spite of the adverse circumstances. They are presented to us as examples.

This truth of having God as the object of faith includes one of the most encouraging facets of the Christian life. It is a cure for that nagging question which constantly plagues the serious Christian regarding the amount and the strength of his faith. When we face a difficult situation we often ask, "I wonder if I have enough faith to cope with this?" or, "Is my faith strong enough to endure?"

The comforting factor in all of this is that such questions are irrelevant. The amount of faith is not the issue. When the Lord Jesus called the faith of the woman of Canaan "great," He was referring to the clear-cut decisions she had made and the persistence with which she maintained them (Matthew 15:21-28). The issue is *not* how we feel about the amount of our faith; it is whether we will exercise faith! It is whether we will make the *right decisions.*

This is also true concerning the strength of faith. Since God is the object of faith, He is the source of faith's strength. The exhortation is, "be strong in the Lord, and in the power of His might" (Ephesians 6:10). When Paul said, "I can do all things through Christ which strengtheneth me" (Philippians 4:13), he was including his ability to believe God. Abraham was commended by God for having a "strong" faith (Romans 4:19, 20). What is meant by this passage is that Abraham made the right decisions in regard to the revealed will of God and persisted in those decisions. The term "strong" is in contrast to the term "weak in faith" in verse 19. There Abraham is commended for not allowing adverse circumstances to hinder his response to the known will of God.

The strength of faith does not reside in the Christian. We may not use the excuse of weakness. When we state or imply, "I didn't have enough faith," or "My faith wasn't strong enough," we are simply blaming God for our failure or we are confessing our ignorance in understanding Biblical faith. When we want to make the right decision of faith and desire to practice the accompanying will of God, we will receive all the strength we need from God!

## THE BIBLICAL EXPLANATION (3):
### Faith has a Context—Love.

In Galatians 5:6, the Apostle Paul stated, "For in Jesus Christ neither circumcision availeth any thing, nor uncircumcision; but *faith which worketh by love.*"

What *does* "avail" to bring the grace and power of God into our lives? By use of the term "circumcision" the Apostle Paul indicated that all the legalism and ceremonialism of the Jewish Christians availed nothing. And by use of the word "uncircumcision" he specified the ecstatic emotional religious experiences of the Gentiles as also unavailing.

We must accept this frank evaluation. No amount of mere rule-keeping, Bible study, church attendance, Christian service, or emotional experience will "avail" in our lives—unless it is a genuine expression of faith and love.

The issue is again shown to be faith. And here we are told that the context of faith, that which makes faith "work," is love. Without love, according to the Apostle Paul, faith does not "work"; it is "inactive."

Now we understand that the correct response to God has two clearly discernible aspects. The two sides to this response are faith and love. Both are necessary. One does not exist without the other. These two are often united in the Bible (1 Corinthians 13:13; 1 Thessalonians 1:3; 1 Timothy 1:5).

What is this love which provides the necessary context for faith? It is love for God! To love God means to give Him His rightful place in our daily life. It is to recognize Him for who He is and to live consistently in harmony with Him. This is the reason why love and obedience are always inseparably related in the Bible (John 14:15; 1 John 5:3).

The failure to love God genuinely is the most serious hindrance to faith in the life of all Christians. We cannot be unconcerned about the will of God and then expect to be able to claim the promises of God. Any and all failures to give God His rightful place strip us of the discernment and ability to make a decision of faith. Because of this truth, the terms "repent" and "confess" are often coupled with the word "believe" in the Bible. Before we can believe, sin—the result of lack of love—must be dealt with.

Faith cannot exist as a daily experience without the reality of love as a daily experience. Faith and love are mutually dependent. This is the answer to the question of why faith is necessary to please God (Hebrews 11:6) and yet love for God is the first commandment (Matthew 22:37, 38).

When we choose to disobey God, by the sin of either commission or omission, we manifest our failure to love Him adequately. Such a choice will leave us without the ability to fellowship with God and to respond to Him by faith. The degree of loss is determined by the seriousness of the choice to disobey.

## THE BIBLICAL EXPLANATION (4):
### Faith has a Basis—the Scripture.

Faith is a decision to respond correctly to God. The content of that decision and response is determined by the Scripture. This is clearly seen in the eleventh chapter of Hebrews. The sacrifice which Abel offered had been specified by God as the only one acceptable. Abel's offering was a *correct response* to God's revelation. Noah built the ark in response to divine directives. Abraham left his homeland and traveled toward Palestine as a response to God's command. The Word of God was the basis of their faith.

In this way faith is rooted in the Scripture. We have been commanded to mix the Word of God with faith (Hebrews 4:1-3). We fulfill the commandment by the persistent effort to put the Word of God into practice in all areas of life as an expression of our love for God.

Our failure to read, to study, and to understand the Scriptures will result in a serious handicap in the expression of our faith and the obedience which should follow. How can we obey God when we do not know His commandments? How can we claim His promises when we do not know their content? How can we believe when we do not know what to believe? (Romans 10:14). "So then faith cometh by hearing, and hearing by the Word of God" (Romans 10:17).

The first step, therefore, toward pleasing God in the expression of faith and love, is an inquiry into the Word of God. Since the Scripture is the basis of our faith, it is necessarily the basis of all of the other facets of our Christian life. Without an understanding of the Word and will of God, grace, peace, power and progress become an impossibility.

The importance of this truth is paramount. No amount of pious effort can be substituted for a simple understanding of the Bible. All efforts to make progress in the Christian life will be thwarted until serious steps are consistently and persistently taken, in becoming familiar with the basic message and themes of the Bible.

## THE BIBLICAL EXHORTATION:
### The Steps in a Decision of Faith.

Progress in the Christian life is usually a step by step process. This is particularly true in the area of sanctification. When we are led by the Holy Spirit to the recognition of some sin in our life, then it is important that we know what to do with that sin. One of the clearest statements in this regard is found in 1 John 1:9, "If we confess our sins, He is faithful and just to forgive us our sins, and to cleanse us from all unrighteousness." In order to mix this Word of God with faith (Hebrews 4:1-3), we must obey God—in a very personal and practical manner—and put the verse into practice.

The first step is to *confess the sin—as* a sin! If we are not willing to do this, there is no need to start praying. No amount of weeping, lamenting, and making of resolutions can take the place of a simple honest confession. When we have disobeyed God and acted out of harmony with His Word, we must in a very specific, pointed, sincere, thorough, and honest way confess our sin for what it really is. We must bluntly name ourselves and our sin. If we have sinned through gossip or doubt or laziness or immorality, we must confess it as such. "Lord, I confess to You that I am a gossip and I have used my tongue to hurt my friend," would be a good way to begin. This confession is a decision, an enactment of faith.

The second step is to *forsake the sin*. This is also a decision. It is the only correct decision which we can make following an acknowledgment of sin. There is no other alternative. This also must be a sincere and honest choice in the presence of God. Any pretense here will destroy all hope of divine help. We must take a stand against our sin and then deliberately and consistently carry out our decision. When Augustine was 32 years old, he suddenly realized the reason he was not a Christian was due to his reluctance to forsake his sin. He confessed that from his early youth he had been praying, "Give me chastity and continency, only not yet" *(Confessions of St. Augustine,* Book VIII, Paragraph 17).

The third step is to *believe God's promise* of forgiveness and cleansing. We must face ourselves with the reality of God's Word and what this verse (1 John 1:9) means today in a very personal and practical way. In the light of our sin, we must come to a clear understanding of what divine forgiveness and cleansing will mean in our lives. And then we must believe God and fully take Him at His Word.

The fourth step is to *receive Jesus Christ* into our lives as the specific cleansing and enablement which our sin demands. Jesus Christ is not only our Savior He is our sanctification and power (1 Corinthians 1:24, 30). In our salvation we made a decision of faith in receiving Him into our lives as our Savior. He came and performed the work of salvation. This initial step in the Christian life is spoken of in the Bible as the blueprint for how we are to progress in daily life (Colossians 2:6). Therefore, when we are in need of a specific cleansing and enablement, it is well to be exact in our decision of faith. If we need help in the area of gossip, it would be well to say, "Heavenly Father, having confessed my sin to You of being a gossipper and having promised to forsake my sin entirely, I do now deliberately and in faith receive Jesus Christ into my life as *my cleansing from gossip* and as *my enablement* to live above this sin."

The fifth step is to *take God at His Word and live accordingly.* He has promised to forgive us and to cleanse us from our sin when we genuinely confess. Having confessed our sin as an act of faith, we must now rely upon the faithfulness and justice of God. If we have confessed, we *are* forgiven and *we have been cleansed.* When temptation comes, as it surely will, we must simply maintain our decision of faith, believing that the sin has already been dealt with, and refuse the temptation. As long as we continue this dependence on God and genuinely desire to be free from that sin, we will have the continuing grace and power of God to be free (John 8:32, 36). The promise of God is clear. He has said that if we respond to Him obediently in faith and love, He will come and work in us by His grace and power (Romans 6:16-18; Philippians 2:12, 13; 1 Peter 1:22).

When you have mastered this lesson, take the first part of Exam 6 (covering lesson 10), questions 1-10 on pages 117-119 (right after lesson 11). Remember, you will not turn this exam in for correction until after you have done lesson 11.

# "And Now Faith Demands..."

## FAITH DEMANDS:
## A Correct Beginning.

In the first chapter we stated that the Christian must learn the truths of Christianity and how to put them into practice. This last chapter is a statement on "practice." It will explain the most important element of "practice" which is a decision of faith. So there will be no misunderstanding, the necessary decisions of faith will be explained and a suggested prayer given.

How does one approach the true and living God? The attitude that just any approach will do could hardly be more incorrect. God is infinite, eternal, and absolute holiness. We can only come to God in the way *He* has specified and ordained. Jesus Christ said, "I am the way, the truth, and the life: no man cometh unto the Father, but by Me" (John 14:6).

The non-Christian may come to God only through Jesus Christ. A correct beginning means a sincere and thorough repentance for sin, a wholehearted surrender to the authority of Jesus Christ and His Word, and a deliberate, specific decision to receive Jesus Christ as Lord and Savior. The following prayer may help:[1]

---

[1] The prayers in this lesson are included as *suggestions* only. Many will prefer to put them into their own words. Obviously the mechanical recital of a written prayer cannot be effective. The desire for a changed life must well up from one's own heart in response to the Spirit's working.

Eternal God, I bow before You in a sincere and honest confession that I am a sinner and that I have sinned against You. I repent of my sin and apologize to You for all I have done. I completely surrender to Your authority and control as You have stated it in the Bible. On the basis of Your Word, Lord Jesus, I do now receive You into my life as my Lord and Savior. I believe in You and accept You as my forgiveness, cleansing, righteousness, and eternal life. I want to thank You for making all of this possible. In Jesus' Name, Amen. (Luke 13:3; Acts 17:30; John 1:12; 3:16-18, 36; 5:24; 8:24; Romans 5:1; 8:1; 10:9, 10; 2 Corinthians 5:21; 1 John 1:9; Revelation 3:20.)

The Christian is in an entirely different relationship to God than the non-Christian. However, we may likewise come to God only through Jesus Christ. As believers, the issue in our lives is no longer that of initial salvation; we have been accepted and forgiven. The issue is now daily obedience.

How are we as Christians to approach God through Jesus Christ? We may come only in the way which is in harmony with the Person of Jesus Christ, His work, and His Word. Who He is, what He has done in history, and what He has said in His Word are the determining factors in our approach to God. A correct beginning, therefore, must be with complete sincerity and honesty. One may not pretend with God! All hypocrisy, sham, platitudes, pride, playing-the-game, and mask-wearing must be deliberately and honestly abandoned. In the place of these, we must decisively surrender *ourselves* to God. We must begin with ourselves, as we bow before God, and acknowledge that all failure in practice is our failure *as a person.* No elusive side-stepping of this basic truth may be tolerated.

However, we must do more than acknowledge our failures of faith and love. To meet the demand of faith, we must put the Word of God into practice. We must, therefore, personally assume the responsibility for being the right kind of person and for living in harmony with the Person, work, and Word of God. No decision is greater nor more important than this. All other correct decisions find their roots here:

Heavenly Father, I bow before You in a sincere and honest choice to surrender myself wholly to You as You have made Yourself known to me in the Holy Scripture. I accept Your Word as my only authoritative standard for all of my life and activity. Therefore, I make the decision not to judge You, Your work, myself, nor others on the basis of my feelings or circumstances. (Romans 12:1, 2; John 15:7, 10; Romans 10:17; 1 Corinthians 4:3-5; 2 Corinthians 10:12.)

## FAITH DEMANDS:
## A Correct Attitude Toward God.

To approach the true and living God correctly, we must come to Him in the attitude of worship and praise. God is worthy of all glory which could be given to Him. The highest deed which can be performed by man and the most essential is that of true worship. To come to God in selfishness, with our minds filled only with our own needs, is not the correct attitude. The reality of the true and living God, who is pure spirit, infinite, eternal and unchangeable in His being, wisdom, power, holiness, truth, and love, should compel us to worship Him with our total being. Any failure to do so indicates our ignorance of the greatness and goodness of the triune God.

The slightest reflection on the greatness of God, as manifested in His work as the Creator and Sustainer of all things, as the Governor of all nations, the Author of history, the Head of the Church, the Lord of the harvest, and the Savior of mankind, should likewise cause us to bow before Him in adoration and praise.

Faith, therefore, demands that we recognize the greatness and goodness of God and worship Him for who He is and what He has done. It may be helpful to use the following affirmation:

I bow to acknowledge that You, the triune God, are worthy of all honor, praise, and worship as the Creator, Sustainer, and End of all things. As my Creator, I recognize that You made me for Yourself. I, therefore, choose to live for You. I am grateful that You loved me and chose me in Jesus Christ in eternity past and proved Your love in sending Your Son to die in my place. I praise You for every provision which has already been made for my past, present, and future needs through the representative work of Jesus Christ in whom I have been quickened, raised, seated in the heavenlies, and anointed with the Holy Spirit. (Revelation 4:11; Romans 12:1, 2; 5:6-11; 8:28-39; Philippians 1:6; 4:6, 7, 13, 19; Ephesians 1:3; 2:5, 6; Acts 2:1-4, 33.)


## FAITH DEMANDS:
### A Correct Understanding of the Permanence of Salvation.

Worshipping and honoring God are not acts performed only on our knees. They involve every part of our life and day. One of the most serious ways in which we dishonor God is to doubt His Word, either through ignorance or, worse yet, through presumptuous choice. A crucial area in this regard has to do with the possession of salvation. Our shallow understanding of the profound depths of divine redemption easily propels us into ingratitude and gnawing doubt. As a result we judge God and evaluate His Work and love on the basis of feeling and circumstance. This we may not do.

It is important to understand the provision God has made for us and to accept decisively as the truth what He has said in His Word concerning our salvation. The following prayer is an illustration of how this may be done:

Since I have received Your Son the Lord Jesus Christ as my Lord and Savior, *I believe Your Word* that You have received me, forgiven me, adopted me into Your family, assumed every responsibility for me, given to me eternal life, and made me complete in Christ. I accept the truth of *Your Word* that the Lord Jesus offers Himself to me as my daily sufficiency through prayer and the decisions of faith, and that the Holy Spirit Himself has baptized me into the Body of Christ, sealed me, anointed me for life and service, seeks to lead me into a deeper walk with the Lord Jesus and to fill my life with Himself. I accept these truths as realities in my life today. (John 1:12; Ephesians 1:6, 7; John 17:11, 17, 21, 24; Ephesians 1:5; Philippians 1:6; John 3:36; 1 John 5:9-13; Colossians 2:10; 1 Corinthians 1:30; Colossians 1:27; Galatians 2:20; John 14:13, 14; Matthew 21:22; Romans 6:1-19; Hebrews 4:1-3; 1 Corinthians 12:13; Ephesians 1:13, 14; Acts 1:8; John 7:37-39; 14:16-18; 15:26, 27; 16:13-15; Romans 8:11-16; Ephesians 5:18.)

# FAITH DEMANDS
## A Correct Evaluation of Sin and Holiness.

To honor and glorify God in daily life, faith demands that we understand and evaluate sin and holiness correctly. The Christian has the awesome ability to obey God and thereby bring holiness into his life, or to disobey God and thereby bring sin into his life. The kind of person we will become in character and practice is determined by the choice we make today. In this regard our future is an undeveloped potentiality for good and evil. Our manner of life in the future is determined by the sort of person we will be and this in turn is determined by our evaluation of sin and holiness today. It is impossible to sin and escape the destructive force sin has upon our character. Likewise, obedience to God will bring strength and virtue of character.

As Christians, therefore, we must take a stand against our own sinful nature and the temptations from without and within. We must choose to live according to the will of God and to be characterized by the holiness which is both the demand and the promise of God.

An important step in this direction is the acknowledgment of our inability to cope with sin and our inability to produce a holy character. The secret of sanctification is not found in our own resolutions or desires; it is found in Jesus Christ and His work within us, through the ministry of the Holy Spirit (1 Corinthians 1:30; Romans 8:1-17):

I acknowledge in Your presence that only You can deal with my sin and only You can produce holiness in my life. In both of these areas I am dependent upon You and Your grace. I, therefore, choose to wholly surrender myself to You to obey Your Word. I recognize that You have made every necessary provision for my daily life so that I may fulfill Your will and call. Therefore, I will not make excuses for my sin and failure. I renounce all self-effort to live the Christian life and to perform Christian service. I renounce all the sinful religious activity which only weeps over sin and failure. I renounce the sinful praying which would ask You to change circumstances and people so that I may be more spiritual. I renounce all drawing back from the work of the Holy Spirit within and the call of God without. And I renounce all those motives, goals, and activities which have served my sinful pride. (1 Corinthians 1:30; 2 Corinthians 9:8; Galatians 2:20; 1 John 5:4; Romans 6:16-20; 1 Thessalonians 5:24.)

# FAITH DEMANDS:
## A Correct Response to the Commands of God.

Faith is essentially a decision, made in dependence upon God, in response to the promises and commands of the Scripture. When such decisions are made and put into practice, the grace of God flows into our lives, and we are increasingly set free from sin and increasingly enabled to live a holy life (Romans 6:11-22; Philippians 2:12, 13; 1 Peter 1:22).

The secret of a successful Christian life is, therefore, rooted in the Word of God and in the believer's sincere response to God and His Word. There is no other place to begin. Everything in practical Christianity begins with God, His Word, and the individual's decision to respond correctly to God. When we know the Biblical commandments regarding personal sanctification, honestly desire to obey God and make the right decisions of faith, then, and only then, will we know the will, grace, and power of God in our daily lives.

The demand of faith, therefore, is three-fold. First, we must know the commands and promises of God. Second, we must possess a sincere and honest desire to obey and believe God. Third, we must acquire the knowledge of how to make a decision of faith and follow through by making such decisions.

In the New Testament there are four basic commands regarding the believer's daily life. All of the other commands and exhortations may be subsumed under these four or may be said to be their fulfillment.

These four commands are the application, in the believer's daily life, of the four historical deeds of redemption upon which all of Christianity rests. What the crucifixion, resurrection, ascension, and Pentecost imply and demand in our daily lives has been summarized into these four specific commands.

Because the Lord Jesus Christ was crucified as our Representative so that we may be cleansed from the power of our sinful fallen nature, we have been commanded to "put off the old man" (Ephesians 4:22):

I now make the decision, Lord Jesus, to own You as my sanctification, particularly now as my cleansing from the old nature, and ask You, blessed Holy Spirit, to apply to me the work of the crucifixion. Cleanse me from my pride, hypocrisy, lust, selfishness, doubt, and jealousy which I confess as sin. In cooperation with and dependence upon You, I make the decision of faith to "put off the old man." (Romans 6:1-22; 1 Corinthians 1:30; Galatians 5:6-21; Ephesians 4:22; Colossians 3:1-17.)

Because the Lord Jesus Christ was resurrected as our Representative so that we may be enabled to live free from sin in holiness of life, we have been commanded to "put on the new man" (Ephesians 4:24):

I now make the decision, Lord Jesus, to own You as my sanctification, particularly now as my enablement moment by moment to live above sin, and I do ask You, blessed Holy Spirit, to apply to me the work of the resurrection so that I may walk in newness of life. I sincerely desire to have humility, honesty, purity, love, faith, and long-suffering in my daily life. In cooperation with and dependence upon You I make the decision of faith to "put on the new man." (Romans 6:1-4; Galatians 5:22-26; Ephesians 4:24.)

Because the Lord Jesus Christ ascended as our Representative to provide deliverance from Satan, we have been commanded to "resist the Devil" (Ephesians 4:27):

I now make the decision, Lord Jesus, to own You as my deliverance from Satan and by faith take my position with You in the heavenlies. I do ask You, blessed Holy Spirit, to apply to me the work of the ascension. I would wholly surrender to You and, in the Name of Jesus Christ, take my stand against all Satanic influence and subtlety. In cooperation with and dependence upon You, I make the decision of faith to "resist the Devil." (Ephesians 1:17-23; 2:1-6; 4:27; 6:10-18; Colossians 1:13; Hebrews 2:14, 15; James 4:7; 1 Peter 5:8, 9.)

Because the Lord Jesus Christ received the Holy Spirit as our Representative and bestowed Him upon His Church, we have been commanded to "be filled with the [Holy] Spirit" (Ephesians 5:18):

I now make the decision to own You, blessed Holy Spirit, as my anointing for every area of my life. I ask You, in all sincerity, to bring my character and life into full conformity to the Person of Jesus Christ and the will of God. Please work with me so that Jesus Christ may be glorified and the fruit of Your presence may be seen in my life. In cooperation with and dependence upon You, I make the decision of faith to be "filled with the [Holy] Spirit." (John 7:37-39; 14:16, 17, 26; 15:26, 27; 16:7-15; Acts 1:8; 2:33; Romans 8:1-17; Ephesians 5:18.)

## FAITH DEMANDS:
### A Correct Dependence Upon the Faithfulness of God.

And now that we have responded to God and have obeyed His commands by making the necessary decisions of faith, what is the next step? It is simply to believe God and to live accordingly. When we are faced with a temptation or choice which would be contradictory to the Person and deeds of God, the Word of God, and our decisions of faith, that form of thinking and acting must be rejected in dependence upon God and as a re-affirmation of our faith. If we have sincerely made the decisions of faith and honestly desire to live accordingly, we can expect the wisdom, grace, and power to live a successful Christian life.

Having made this confession and these decisions of faith, I now take as my own Your promised rest for this day. I relax in the trust of faith knowing that in the moment of temptation, trial, or need, You will be there to be my strength and sufficiency. (Hebrews 4:1-13; 1 Corinthians 10:13.)

For the sake of clarity and convenience, the prayers given above are here compiled with some amplification. The Bible references are presented so the various concepts may be found in the Scripture and utilized for further study.

When you are ready, complete Exam 6 by answering questions 11-20 on pages 119-121. (You should have already answered questions 1-10 as part of your study of lesson 10.)

When you have answered all the questions in Exam 6, mail the exam for correction.

# HIGHER GROUND

Name_____ 
(print plainly)

Exam
Grade_____

Address _____

City_____ State _____ Zip Code _____ Class Number _____

Instructor _____

## LESSON 10

*In the blank space in the right-hand margin write the letter of the correct answer.*

**1.** Which of the following best describes faith? It is
   a. the feeling of well-being which results from a positive response to religious truth
   b. an abstract concept, difficult to define but generally associated with a religious creed or philosophy of life
   c. a virtue, stronger in some than in others, but in any case very difficult to acquire
   d. a deliberate act of submission to God and trust in His Son          _____

**2.** A study of Hebrews 11 reveals that every person mentioned in that chapter as exhibiting faith also manifested, as part of that faith,
   a. an attitude of self-confidence
   b. a characteristic of obedience
   c. a spirit of independence
   d. a trait of indecision
   e. the ability to grasp abstract ideas          _____

**3.** When considering faith, the vital thing to weigh is
   a. the amount of faith a person has
   b. that faith makes it possible for us to believe things which are contrary to reason
   c. that faith's object is God Himself
   d. that faith is very exclusive and is possessed in any appreciable degree by only a few          _____

4. Abraham is set forth in Scripture as an example of a man
   a. strong in faith
   b. weak in faith
   c. both weak and strong in faith
   d. of average faith
   _____

5. According to Galatians 5:6, faith can be made to work in our lives only as a result of
   a. practice
   b. determination
   c. love
   d. experience
   _____

6. The most serious hindrance to faith in the life of a Christian is the failure to
   a. attend church regularly
   b. witness for Christ consistently
   c. pray adequately
   d. love God genuinely
   _____

7. According to Romans 10:17
   a. faith comes by hearing God's Word
   b. the Word of God must be mixed with faith if it is to bear practical fruit in the life
   c. faith is essential if we are to please God
   d. faith may be either "strong" or "weak"
   _____

8. In order to make faith grow it is necessary to
   a. know God's commandments and promises
   b. become familiar with the basic message and themes of the Bible
   c. read, study and understand the Scriptures
   d. do all the above
   _____

9. St. Augustine testified that
   a. he never had any aspirations after holiness in his early youth
   b. he always believed, even in his early youth, but never really amounted to anything as a Christian until he attended church regularly
   c. the reason he did not become a Christian in his youth could be traced to his reluctance to forsake his sin
   d. as a youth he prayed: "Give me chastity or give me death"
   _____

**10.** When we confess sin and failure as an act of faith we
   a. next rely on God in an attitude of continual dependence for grace and power to live in freedom from sin
   b. experience permanent emancipation from sin in all its forms
   c. thereafter forget sin since its power is broken and its attractiveness dispelled
   d. need to anxiously watch lest we fall into temptation again and sin once more for only at the cost of constant vigilance can we be sure of never sinning again

## WHAT DO YOU SAY?

Describe one way in which you have put faith to work in your life.

_____

_____

_____

_____

_____

## LESSON 11

*In the blank space in the right-hand margin write the letter of the correct answer.*

**11.** In John 14:6 the Lord Jesus declared that He is THE way to God. This statement
   a. applies to non-Christians only
   b. applies to Christians only
   c. applies both to Christians and non-Christians
   d. is too dogmatic since there are no such absolutes          _____

**12.** The most important decision a person can make once he has become a Christian, a decision which will control and condition all other decisions, is the decision to
   a. attend church regularly and have fellowship with other Christians
   b. be baptized
   c. study the Bible and pray
   d. be the kind of person God wants at all costs          _____

13. The highest and noblest occupation in which a Christian can engage is that of
    a. serving the cause of Christ
    b. becoming a full-time missionary or minister of the gospel
    c. interceding at the throne of God for the salvation and blessing of others
    d. bowing before God in adoring wonder and worship _____

14. To doubt one's salvation is
    a. natural and to be expected
    b. dishonoring to God
    c. a sure sign that sin has come in and severed fellowship with God
    d. an indication that one needs to be saved again _____

15. When confronted with the problem of our sinful nature we should
    a. take a stand against it
    b. choose to live according to God's will
    c. confess our inability to deal with sin and our inability to live a holy life
    d. do all the above _____

16. The only place to begin putting into practice the principles of holy living is with
    a. God and His Word
    b. a solemn resolution to live a holy life
    c. a public act of committal such as a response to an "altar call"
    d. prayer and fasting _____

17. Which of the following is true?
    a. It is immaterial whether or not the cardinal doctrines of Christianity have historical foundation since the Christian philosophy is of a spiritual nature and deals with eternal verities
    b. Such facts as the crucifixion, resurrection and ascension of Christ and the events of Pentecost are significant for the lost since they point to the way of salvation but they have a theological significance only once a person has accepted Christ
    c. Christianity rests upon certain historical certainties the practical fruits of which must be claimed by the Christian and applied to his daily life
    d. Only Pentecost is relevant for the believer desiring to live a holy life; the crucifixion, resurrection and ascension are salvation truths and apply to the lost _____

**18.** The principle and practice of living a victorious Christian life may be summed up *best* in the words
   a. "Joy to the world, the Lord is come"
   b. "Just as I am, I come"
   c. "Trust and obey"
   d. "Jesus keep me near the cross"                    _____

**19.** Which of the following is fatal to a life pleasing to God?
   a. Examining oneself in the light of the Word of God to see if there is any area where the Holy Spirit is being grieved
   b. Deliberately choosing to submit oneself fully to God
   c. Judging God, His work or oneself or others on the basis of feelings or circumstances
   d. None of the above                                 _____

**20.** Where does it say that the Lord Himself will be the strength and sufficiency of those who trust Him even in the moment of temptation, trial and need? In
   a. Isaiah 53:6
   b. Romans 6:23
   c. 1 Corinthians 10:13
   d. Revelation 3:20                                   _____

## WHAT DO YOU SAY?

How has this course helped you?

_____

_____

_____

_____

_____

*MAIL TO address shown on back outside cover.*
*PLEASE enclose a stamped addressed envelope for the return of your corrected exam.*

# THE DAILY AFFIRMATION OF FAITH[1]

Today I deliberately choose to submit myself fully to God as He has made Himself known to me through the Holy Scriptures which I honestly accept as the only inspired, infallible, authoritative standard for all of life and practice. In this day I will not judge God, His work, myself, or others on the basis of feelings or circumstances.

1.  I recognize by faith that the triune God is worthy of all honor, praise, and worship as the Creator, Sustainer, and End of all things. I confess that God, as my Creator, made me for Himself. In this day I therefore choose to live for Him (Revelation 5:9, 10; Isaiah 43:1, 7, 21; Revelation 4:11).

2.  I recognize by faith that God loved me and chose me in Jesus Christ before time began (Ephesians 1:1-7).

3.  I recognize by faith that God has proven His love to me in sending His Son to die in my place, in whom every provision has already been made for my past, present, and future needs through His representative work, and that I have been quickened, raised, seated with Jesus Christ in the heavenlies, and anointed with the Holy Spirit (Romans 5:6-11; 8:28-39; Philippians 1:6; 4:6, 7, 13, 19; Ephesians 1:3; 2:5, 6; Acts 2:1-4, 33).

4.  I recognize by faith that God has accepted me, since I have received Jesus Christ as my Lord and Savior (John 1:12; Ephesians 1:6); that He has forgiven me (Ephesians 1:7); adopted me into His family, assuming every responsibility for me (John 17:11, 17; Ephesians 1:5; Philippians 1:6); given me eternal life (John 3:36; 1 John 5:9-13); applied the perfect righteousness of Christ to me so that I am now justified (Romans 5:1; 8:3, 4; 10:4); made me complete in Christ (Colossians 2:10); and offers *Himself* to me as

---

[1]This prayer is included as *suggestive* only. Many will prefer to put it into their own words. Obviously the mechanical recital of a written prayer cannot be effective. The desire for a changed life must well up from one's own heart in response to the Spirit's working.

my daily sufficiency through prayer and the decisions of faith (1 Corinthians 1:30; Colossians 1:27; Galatians 2:20; John 14:13, 14; Matthew 21:22; Romans 6:1-19; Hebrews 4:1-3.)

5. I recognize by faith that the Holy Spirit has baptized me into the Body of Christ (1 Corinthians 12:13); sealed me (Ephesians 1:13, 14); anointed me for life and service (Acts 1:8; John 7:37-39); seeks to lead me into a deeper walk with Jesus Christ (John 14:16-18; 15:26, 27; 16:13-15; Romans 8:11-16); and to fill my life with Himself (Ephesians 5:18).

6. I recognize by faith that only God can deal with sin and only God can produce holiness of life. I confess that in my salvation my part was only to receive Him and that He dealt with my sin and saved me. Now I confess that in order to live a holy life, I can only surrender to His will and receive Him as my sanctification; trusting Him to do whatever may be necessary in my life, without and within, so I may be enabled to live today in purity, freedom, rest, and power for His glory (John 1:12; 1 Corinthians 1:30; 2 Corinthians 9:8; Galatians 2:20; Hebrews 4:9; 1 John 5:4; Jude 24).

Having confessed that God is worthy of all praise, that the Scriptures are the only authoritative standard, that only God can deal with sin and produce holiness of life, I again recognize my total dependence upon Him and submission to Him. I accept the truth that praying in faith is absolutely necessary for the realization of the will and grace of God in my daily life (1 John 5:14, 15; James 1:6; 4:2, 3; 5:16-18; Philippians 4:6, 7; Hebrews 4:1-13; 11:6, 24-28).

Recognizing that faith is a total response to God by which the daily provisions the Lord has furnished in Himself are appropriated—*I, therefore, make the following decisions of faith:*

1. *For this day* (Hebrews 3:7, 13, 15; 4:7) I make the decision of faith to surrender wholly to the authority of God as He has revealed Himself in the Scripture—*to obey Him.* I confess my sin, face the sinful reality of my old nature, and deliberately choose

to walk in the light, in step with Christ, throughout the hours of this day (Romans 6:16-20; Philippians 2:12, 13; 1 John 1:7, 9).

2. *For this day* I make the decision of faith to surrender wholly to the authority of God as revealed in the Scripture—*to believe Him.* I accept only His Word as final authority. I now believe that since I have confessed my sin, He has forgiven and cleansed me (1 John 1:9). I accept at full value His Word of promise, to be my sufficiency and rest, and will conduct myself accordingly (Exodus 33:14; 1 Corinthians 1:30; 2 Corinthians 9:8; Philippians 4:19).

3. *For this day* I make the decision of faith to recognize that God has made every provision so that I may fulfill His will and calling. Therefore, I will not make any excuse for my sin and failure (1 Thessalonians 5:24).

4. *For this day* I make the decision of faith deliberately to receive from God that provision which He has made for me. I renounce all self-effort to live the Christian life and to perform God's service; renounce all sinful activity which only weeps over sin and failure; renounce all sinful praying which asks God to change circumstances and people so that I may be more spiritual; renounce all drawing back from the work of the Holy Spirit within and the call of God without; and renounce all non-Biblical motives, goals and activities which serve my sinful pride.

   a. I now sincerely own Jesus Christ as my sanctification, particularly as my cleansing from the old nature, and ask the Holy Spirit to apply to me the work Christ accomplished for me in the crucifixion. In cooperation with and dependence upon Him, I obey the command to "put off the old man" (Romans 6:1-14; 1 Corinthians 1:30; Galatians 6:14; Ephesians 4:22).

   b. I now sincerely own Jesus Christ as my sanctification, particularly as my enablement moment by moment to live above sin, and ask the Holy Spirit to apply to me the work of the resurrection so that I may walk in newness of life. I confess that only God can deal with my sin and only God can produce holiness and the fruit of the Spirit in my life. In cooperation with and dependence upon Him, I obey the command to "put on the new man" (Romans 6:1-4; Ephesians 4:24).

c. I now sincerely receive Jesus Christ as my deliverance from Satan and take my position with Him in the heavenlies, asking the Holy Spirit to apply to me the work of the ascension. In His Name I submit myself to God and stand against all Satanic influence and subtlety. In cooperation with and dependence upon God, I obey the command to "resist the Devil" (Ephesians 1:20-23; 2:5, 6; 4:27; 6:10-18; Colossians 1:13; Hebrews 2:14, 15; James 4:7; 1 Peter 3:22; 5:8, 9).

d. I now sincerely own the Holy Spirit as my anointing for every aspect of life and service for today. I fully open my life to Him to fill me afresh in obedience to the command to "be filled with the [Holy] Spirit" (Ephesians 5:18; John 7:37-39; 14:16, 17, 26; 15:26, 27; 16:7-15; Acts 1:8).

Having made this confession and these decisions of faith, I now receive God's promised rest for this day (Hebrews 4:1-13). Therefore, I rest in the trust of faith, knowing that in the moment of temptation, trial, or need, the Lord Himself will be there as my strength and sufficiency (1 Corinthians 10:13).

# NOTES

# NOTES

# NOTES

# NOTES

# NOTES

# NOTES